AFRAID

AFRAID

Understanding the Purpose of Fear and Harnessing the Power of Anxiety

Arash Javanbakht, MD

ROWMAN & LITTLEFIELD
Lanham • Boulder • New York • London

Published by Rowman & Littlefield
An imprint of The Rowman & Littlefield Publishing Group, Inc.
4501 Forbes Boulevard, Suite 200, Lanham, Maryland 20706
www.rowman.com

86-90 Paul Street, London EC2A 4NE

British Library Cataloguing in Publication Information Available

Library of Congress Cataloging-in-Publication Data

978-1-5381-7038-0 (cloth)
978-1-5381-7039-7 (electronic)

To those who were scared, but their actions were fearless.

Contents

Introduction

One of my clearest childhood memories is from the day I was on top of a small ladder I had climbed earlier with my mom. When it was time to climb down, I found myself terrified; I could not even look down. I remember the time of day, the weather, the texture of the ladder, and that only my mother's kind and smiling face, standing at the bottom, could convince me to slowly step on the ladder. That was one of my first encounters with intense fear.

Years later, I rode a mule to the bottom of the Grand Canyon, and sustained 5G force doing rolls in a fighter jet.

There are very few of us who have not woken up screaming from a nightmare. About a third of the world's population suffers from an anxiety disorder, and half of Americans have had at least one traumatic experience like rape, assault, shooting, or natural disaster. Ongoing wars and conflicts have terrorized 1 percent of the world's population into leaving their homes and countries. Regardless of your political affiliation, when you finish watching your favorite cable news, you are left more scared and angry, feeling that not just the US but the whole world is going down in flames. In social media, people are too scared of the "others," and digital tribes have lined up against each other. Even when in love, we are often afraid of losing it, or too much intimacy. Fear and anxiety are with us anywhere we go.

On the other hand, we dedicate a holiday to celebrate fear, and horror movies sell billions. Many of us love to go to haunted houses, or the thrill of bungee jumping or watching someone walk on a tightrope. There is no nation whose folk stories and mythology are not filled with demons and witches and monsters, or does not have elegant art pieces about human's deepest and most archaic emotion.

Fear is arguably as old as life. It is one of the most deeply rooted biological mechanisms that has evolved over hundreds of millions of years in the brains and bodies of animals and humans with one key mission: to increase our chance of survival. Fear is deeply woven in our biology, cultures, politics, and day-to-day life. It was meant to be our closest friend, but has become an

annoying enemy that causes debilitating anxieties in modern life. We sometimes don't even know what we are afraid of. What we for sure know is that
we are afraid too often.

But why are we so scared? How does fear work in our brains? Why does
our body react the way it does when we are scared? What is the evolutionary
purpose of fear, and how is that different or similar in us compared to other
animals? Why do we like to be scared, and pay to watch a horror movie? How
does the brain of a brave person work differently than other people's? How
do we learn to be afraid of the things we should run away from, and how can
we unlearn fears that we do not need or want anymore? Is fear good or bad
for creativity? Can we use fear to our advantage?

What do our nightmares tell us? How do our childhood experiences define
what we fear as adults? How do fear and trauma affect our cultures, and our
genes? Why do we remember the details of our most painful experiences, or
sometimes completely forget them? What does too much fear do to our brains
and bodies? What is trauma, and how can we get rid of its haunting effects?
What are the new technologies and treatments available for phobias, anxiety,
and PTSD, and how do they work? How should I protect myself and my family from the terrible news in the media? What are the tricks political leaders
use to manipulate us without us even knowing?

This book attempts to answer all the above questions. It is a comprehen-
sive review of fear and anxiety, covering most tangible aspects of fear in the
human life. The target audience for this book is the public. Mental health
professionals, psychiatrists, psychologists, neuroscientists, anthropologists,
and those interested in the intersection between culture, politics, and fear will
also find it useful.

I am a psychiatrist and neuroscientist specializing in research and treatment
of fear, anxiety, and trauma. But my contemplation of the roots of fear goes
much further than my medical school training. Since I was a teenager, I've
been curious about what determines human emotions and behavior. In seeking the answer, I read philosophy, religion, and psychology. When I entered
medical school, I became fascinated with how the brain and the behavior
interact, and how subtle changes in the structure or function of the brain can
change the way we feel, think, or behave. That led me to choosing psychiatry
as a specialty. During my psychiatry training, I read the works of Sigmund
Freud and Carl Jung in parallel with neuroscience of the fear networks in
the brain.

After finishing my psychiatry residency and fellowship at the University
of Michigan, I went to Wayne State University to found the Stress, Trauma,
and Anxiety Research Clinic (STARC). I had noticed that researchers and
clinicians worked mostly separate from each other, without cutting-edge
research being used much in the clinical world. STARC had two missions:

to bring clinical wisdom to research, and research insight to clinical work. Near a decade later, STARC is now internationally recognized for our work in research and treatment of trauma and anxiety. We research how trauma and stress change our bodies, brains, and genes. We also work on advancing cutting-edge treatment methods, including highly innovative augmented reality technologies and telemedicine. In my clinic, I work with patients with all sorts of anxieties, survivors of torture and human trafficking, refugees, and first responders. I have found helping anxious and traumatized people abundantly fulfilling, and human's ability for recovery fascinating. I also find enormous satisfaction in public scholarly work.

In October 2017, I was asked to write a public education piece for The Conversation (https://theconversation.com/us) about why we love to be scared, to be punished before Halloween. "The Science of Fright: Why We Love to Be Scared" was the first scientific article I wrote specifically for the public. By now, that piece has been read by millions, and I have done tens of radio and TV interviews about it. "The Science of Fright" was a defining moment in my career when I recognized how impactful talking to the public can be. While the result of my research (whose importance I do not deny) only reaches a small number of scientists specialized in my field, good public scholarly work has the potential for educating millions of people. Especially in this age of misinformation, partial science, and pseudoscience, I find it crucial to provide the public with the facts in a fun and understandable, still scientifically solid way. This book is an effort in doing exactly that.

What you will read in this book is the result of two decades of my clinical work and research, and the work of others, from Freud to contemporary neuroscientists. I have shared selected stories from thousands of patients I have worked with, and what I and other scientists have learned from looking at brains of people who were anxious or traumatized. Some of this work is an extension of what I have shared with the public in written media, and the result of conversations with other scientists, and reporters who have interviewed me on some of the subjects covered in this book. Their thoughtful questions aimed at what is interesting to the public have helped me formulate the answers in an engaging and interesting way.

I have tried my best to avoid boring science jargon. This is in part thanks to my wife, who kept reminding me that research details that matter to my scientist colleagues are not always interesting to a reader who is not a neuroscientist. I kept that advice in mind as I was writing each sentence of this book. I have also avoided the pop psychology style of exaggerating the facts and offering partially scientific claims. I have stood on solid scientific ground of evidence-based neuroscience, psychology, and psychiatry research, and experience from clinical practice. I made sure to use many examples from palpable clinical and research experiences that most readers can relate to. I agree with Albert Einstein that "example isn't another way to teach, it is the only way to teach." To keep the anonymity of the patients whose cases are shared in this book, I have changed their genders, names, ages, jobs, and other characteristics that might lead to their identification.

Out of respect for the reader's time, I have avoided beating around the bush, too much autobiographical stories, and uninteresting research method details, and have just offered the core and gist of the concepts that matter. While avoiding the shallow "self-help" approach, throughout the chapters of this book I have provided practical tips on how to overcome anxieties of the discussed topics. Sometimes that is simply by explaining how and why we feel nervous in certain situations. My hope is that not only you will enjoy reading this book, but you will also learn about yourself, those around you, your society, and adaptive ways of protecting yourself and your loved ones from unnecessary fear and anxiety.

This book would not be possible without the selfless dedication of my parents, who worked very hard and prioritized their children's education and prosperity. It is also owed to those who mentored me in the way of life and science, and the funders including the National Institutes of Health who have supported my research. I am thankful to those scientists whose shoulders I have stood on, and scientists and trainees at STARC who have worked tirelessly to bring my research ideas and studies to fruition. Most importantly I should thank the patients who have been my best mentors and teachers. They taught me most of what I know about fear, trauma, and anxiety, and humans' immense ability for recovery. I also thank my wife who walked with me through this journey and kept me connected to realities of what a reader would want from this book.

And finally, thank you for giving meaning to this work!

Arash Javanbakht, MD,
November 30, 2022,
a resort near the mountains in Tucson, Arizona

Chapter 1

The Origin of Fear

Evolved to be Scared

The cave you fear to enter holds the treasure you seek.

—Joseph Campbell

FEAR IS AS OLD AS LIFE

Fear is arguably as old as life. It is one of the most original and deeply rooted biological mechanisms that can be traced to the oldest forms of life. It has evolved over hundreds of millions of years with one key mission: to protect the organisms against annihilation and to increase their chance of survival. Fear can be as primitive as the cringe of the antenna of a snail when touched, and as complicated and abstract as the existential fears of humans. It is one of our most fundamental and intimate emotional experiences, deeply rooted in our psychological and biological being. We experience fear with all our mind and body. Except those with damage to certain areas of the brain, we are all familiar with the unpleasant experience of anxiety, focused attention on the perceived danger and distraction from everything else, dry mouth, sweaty hands, rapid heart rate, and tightness in the chest and the stomach that accompany this emotion. Fear is deeply intertwined with the human life and colors our literature, culture, politics, art, and folklore.

Fear is one of the least controllable emotions and is often hard to suppress or hide. When we are scared, all of our being speaks and hears the language of fear.

Fear is defined as a disturbing emotion, and the consequent mental and physiological conscious and unconscious reactions to the perception of threat.

1

Such threat could be real, imaginary, internal, or external. We might be afraid of a predator approaching us, the monsters and demons we have heard about in myths or seen in the movies, our own obsessive thoughts that our loved ones might fall prey to an illness, or news we have heard about a deadly illness spread by a pandemic. As humans, we are also able to be afraid of abstract concepts, things, or people we have never encountered in our own lives. Fear can be productive, counterproductive, and often misguided and abused. Fear can save our life by triggering rapid reactions moving us away from a fast-approaching car, or hurt us, others, or our opportunities by causing hatred for people of a race, nationality, or religion because we were told they are dangerous. We can be afraid of something in our immediate physical and temporal vicinity, or something far distant in the future or even the past.

In all these cases, the function of the emotion of fear and the behaviors it triggers is protecting us against what is perceived as dangerous, whether it is real or an imagination created by ourselves or others.

FEAR VERSUS ANXIETY

There are different words used to describe that unpleasant feeling we experience when facing or anticipating danger. The two commonly used terms in psychology and neuroscience are fear and anxiety. Although these two words are often used interchangeably and largely overlap, there is some difference in their source, as well as mental, brain, and physiological functions triggered by each of them. Fear is a response to a known, clearly defined external threat; for example, a gun is pointed at us or a predator approaching us. In that sense, fear is targeted, often short lived, and disappears as soon as the threat is removed.

Anxiety, on the other hand, is a response to an unknown and vague threat, often has an internal source, and involves a diffuse sense of apprehension. While a gun that is pointed at us triggers fear, what we experience when we learn that a murderer is on the loose in the neighborhood is anxiety. We do not exactly know where the danger is or when we might face it, but we know it could confront us at some point in an undetermined place. In summary, fear prepares us to combat or avoid the immediate threat, whereas anxiety creates a state of vigilance and prepares us to fend off uncertain and unclear threat and danger.

When scared, we focus all our attention and mental and physical resources on the perceived threat, to fight it or escape from it. When anxious, we are in a constant state of alertness and keep screening the environment for an unknown or less known threat. Anxiety often has an internal origin without a necessary and obvious source of danger outside our head. For example, we may experience a sense of dread and apprehension without even knowing what we are afraid of—we just feel it inside our mind and our body. That is anxiety.

In psychiatry, examples of fear-related mental disorders are phobias—for example, fear of dogs or snakes. On the other hand, anxiety-related disorders involve a vague sense of constant anxiety, or worrying about a lot of things, real or imagined, or literally everything potentially going wrong, in what is called generalized anxiety disorder. In chapters 8 and 9 I will delve deeper into the diseases of fear and anxiety.

EVOLUTIONARY FUNCTION OF FEAR

I always tell my patients and students, "To understand fear, we need to know its evolutionary purpose." Otherwise, a lot of fear reactions in our mind and body do not make much sense in the context of modern human society. For example, giving a public talk scares many of us. The feelings of chest tightness, shortened breath, and pounding heart, and distracted attention are most uncomfortable if not counterproductive, are at least not helpful in giving a good public presentation. In modern life, very often fear and anxiety do not help us. They only limit our ability to do well in an exam, job interview, or a presentation to the class. But it just does not make sense that a reaction that is supposed to help and protect us is hurting us and our opportunities more often than not. The reason is, the environment in which our fear system evolved was very different than that of our current modern life.

Fear has been around for as long as animal life has existed, and has evolved very slowly to help organisms adapt to the harsh nature of their environment. As with most other changes in nature, the evolution of fear networks in the brain, and related physiological reactions inside the body, have been so slow and tightly knit among different species that humans abundantly share these networks and reactions with other more primitive animals. These similarities are so large that neuroscientists and psychologists research the brain and behavior of rats and mice to learn about and model our own fear. Interestingly, the more basic a mental function (such as fear, addiction, or pleasure), the more similarities exist between us and less evolved animals.

From an evolutionary standpoint, the most important functions of organisms are self-preservation and procreation. For a nonsocial primitive animal, these functions include eating and not being eaten, or killed by the competitors, finding a mate, and feeding and protecting the offspring. In more complicated and evolved animals with social and group functions (such as chimpanzees and apes), the ability to ally with one's own pack or tribe against the outside forces, and the ability to detect signs of anger or fear in one's groupmates become crucial for survival. It is specifically important to be able to know when other group members are scared, and look for the source of the danger to the group. It is also important to know when one's group members or those from the other groups are angry, because that might mean a need to fight them or just back off. A lot of the same applied to our ancestors. Fifty thousand years ago, survival highly depended on our ability to protect ourselves, our children, and our tribemates against death, injury, or hunger. The danger could come from nature, predators, rival tribes, and often our own tribemates. To handle these threats, we needed to react very fast, and to physically ward off the threat or escape from it. These functions would require physical preparedness and intense focus on the perceived threat. To run away from a predator or fight a warrior from a rival tribe, we needed our heart to pump blood faster to our muscles, and our lungs to increase our oxygen supply. Many of these reactions mismatch the needs of the modern life and end up being more distracting than helpful.

Common observable fear reactions fall within three categories shared among different species: fight, flight, and freezing. Most people are familiar with the concept of "fight or flight" and the associated "adrenaline rush." With profound changes in the brain and the body functions, which I will explain in the next two chapters, animals increase their ability for focused mental and physical activity that allows them to engage in self-defense, or fending off the threat. They may also try to avoid the danger by fleeing it. Flight is especially useful when the risk of death or injury is high, or the subject of the conflict (e.g., food) is not worthy to justify those risks. If avoiding the threat is not possible or is costly, usually the "fight" mode is activated to try to repel or damage the source of danger. A choice between fight and flight is complicated and depends on the species (a gazelle more often engages in flight, and a lion chooses fight/attack); the dynamics between the parties engaged; the resources available; and the current level of energy and strength, injury, and preparedness for defense. While interacting with the enemy, via complicated dynamic and rapid calculations, each animal may repeatedly shift between these two modes. In the commonly known example, while a cat more often decides to avoid a hostile larger animal by running away from it, when cornered, it is more likely to launch an attack as the last self-defense option. These dynamics also explain the interesting and deep relationship between fear and aggression as the two sides of the same coin, which I will delineate in chapter 7.

Freezing is another fear reaction with which humans are less familiar. This fear response more evidently happens in other animals that are less capable of fighting, like mice and rabbits. During the freezing, the animal is immobile yet attentive, with a defensive muscle tone and posture, and reduced vocalization. While fight-or-flight response is accompanied by an increased sympathetic activation that leads to increased heart rate and blood pressure, during the freezing, parasympathetic nervous system activation reduces heart rate and shuts down the fight-or-flight-related behaviors. Freezing's main function is to allow the animal to hide from the predator. The choice between fleeing or freezing not only depends on the species, but also the proximity of the predator or danger, and the available routes to escape. Freezing may switch to fleeing as the predator nears the prey, indicating the prey is identified, or when escape routes seem to be more available. A rabbit freezing at the sight of a hawk will make it more difficult for the hawk to detect it by blending in with the environment more effectively. During freezing, the rabbit will also be dynamically processing the approach of the hawk, and potential routes of escape and the most energy economic ones, to save the vital energy that will be dearly needed when the hawk comes too close.

Freezing response is more complicated in humans and often shows itself in the form of immobility; a pause in decision-making; or dissociation during intense, immediate, and close encounter with life-threatening danger. Dissociation is when the person becomes detached from important elements of the environment, including their own sense of pain, distracting them from the most painful aspects of the experience. Freezing in humans often happens when escape from the danger is impossible, and struggling only increases risk of serious injury and death. As a last resort, freezing aims at increasing the likelihood of survival, and conserving the vital resources for the moment that might come up with a possibility of fleeing or neutralizing the danger. Freezing is often seen in victims of serious abuse, torture, or rape, when the most self-preserving automatic response is immobility. I have often heard from survivors of such horrible experiences that their body automatically and without their volition had shut down and become immobile, and they lost the ability to think clearly or fight off the perpetrator. Dissociation is often an element of this phenomenon, and feels like the person is detached from their body, is not mentally fully there, or is semiconscious.

FEAR AND MODERN LIFE

In the example of anxiety when giving a public speech, the person is disturbed and distracted by pounding heart, shortness of breath, sweaty body, and poor concentration. These bodily changes make more sense in the context of the evolution of fear. Fifty thousand years ago, if we were talking to a group of our tribemates and they did not like us, chances were high that one of us would be dead or highly injured in a matter of minutes. In that sense, the fight-or-flight bodily reactions were needed for self-preservation. When we are giving a talk, the same primitive brain is reacting to the perception of potential social threat by preparing the body for fight or flight. The problem here is that our physiology changes and evolves much more slowly than our social environment and civilization. While our brain hardware has not changed much over the past tens of thousands of years, our environment has. In the modern-life context, the worst thing that can happen if the people you are presenting to do not like you or your talk is that they will not ask you to talk for them again, or you might get a lower grade on an evaluation. But the brain perceives a socially challenging context today, the same way it would a hundred thousand years ago. It is as if there is still an ape sitting inside of us, reacting the way it should in life in the jungle.

This happens too often in our day-to-day life. Sometimes when we are expecting a stressful meeting with our boss or professor, the same intense feelings, thoughts, physical reactions, and sense of doom appear the days and nights before the anticipated meeting, the feelings we would have if we were anticipating a fight or a battle. The reason is that in the natural context of our evolution, if the head of the tribe or a warlord did not like the anticipated interaction, we would have a chance of facing serious injury, death, deprivation, or exile.

Overall, modern life has turned a very important evolutionary warning system into a false alarm. The fear system that used to save our lives and help us survive at a personal and collective level frequently misunderstands our current circumstances and triggers responses that are adaptive only for the life of a primitive human. On the other hand, as the likelihood of serious traditional dangers like war, predators, and natural disasters are decreased, we rarely experience fear in the settings it has evolved for. Like we do not use our muscles the way they evolved to be used, we do not use our fear system naturally. This causes us challenges, confusion, and maladaptive anxieties. I will discuss this angle more in the later chapters.

I in no way mean to say fear is totally unnecessary and irrelevant these days. Research has shown animals that are unable to experience fear due to damage in brain fear processing areas are more likely to be killed or injured by others. Fear and the associated fast reactions and behaviors still serve us during wars, assaults, natural disasters, encounter with a fast-approaching car, or an angry dog. In clinical practice, it is important to have a good understanding of how fear and anxiety function as a false alarm in some mental disorders. But we also know fear is still often a valuable mechanism to protect us from harm. I educate my trainees that fear and anxiety sometimes are simply the pin in the wrong chair we are sitting on, to inform us that we must leave that chair, that job, or that abusive relationship. As I will explain in chapters 8 and 9, fear and anxiety are abnormal when they are not adaptive and cause debilitating levels of unhelpful distress, dysfunction, or both.

INNATE VERSUS LEARNED, CONCRETE
VERSUS ABSTRACT FEAR

Sources of fear and anxiety can be very diverse in form and complexity. The simplest and most concrete form is an external obvious object, for example, a wolf approaching. This fear can be known inherently, or learned from others. For example, someone can tell us this is a friendly pet dog that looks like a wolf, or inversely, that this dog hates strangers. Fear could also be caused by interaction between the object and our thoughts and previous experiences, for example, that a dog could be contaminated with a dangerous disease, or memories that a dog attacked a sibling when we were a child. That dog could resemble a vicious dog we saw in a movie when we were younger. I have seen patients who were too afraid of spiders, sharks, or clowns after they saw the movies *Tarantula, Jaws*, and *It* in their childhood. Our thoughts, for example, anticipation of something bad happening, could also cause anxiety, for instance, fear of a loved one having a car accident when on a road trip. In a patient with obsessive-compulsive disorder, anxiety is caused by the repeated thought of having not turned off the stove and that the house will burn to the ground.

Sometimes what scares us is complicated and abstract, or of existential nature. Even other feelings can trigger complicated and less concrete fears. People can fear punishment by God or the universe because of guilt they have about something wrong they have done years ago. In the Freudian psycho-analytic approach, fear and anxiety result from internal conflict between con-tradicting desires. For example, *castration anxiety* is fear of being punished because of a boy's fantasies of competition with father, to win mother's love. Just the mere presence of such fantasies, some of them unconscious, could cause anxiety, even years after father is gone. Because of its unconscious nature, sometimes the anxiety is felt without even knowing why it is there. In chapters 8, 9, and 10, I will in more detail explain the disorders of fear and anxiety.

While most of our fears are learned from experience or from others, there are some fears we are born with, or we are more susceptible to develop. Like some behaviors that are engraved in our genetic codes as humans, there are fears that we are born with. Some examples are fear of predators, loud noises, heights, snakes, spiders, and rapidly approaching objects. From an evolution-ary standpoint, these dangers are so common and detrimental to the species' survival that those with a genetic tendency to avoid them had a higher likeli-hood of surviving and transferring their genes to the upcoming generations.

MODERATORS OF FEAR AND ANXIETY

Multiple factors determine the intensity of fear or anxiety in the face of a unique danger. These factors in different circumstances (or different people) impact the level of fear experienced, and consequent fear-related behaviors.

Perceived Threat

One of my favorite movies is *Life Is Beautiful*, the excellent work of Italian director and actor Roberto Benigni. In this movie, Guido and his family are placed in a concentration camp. To reduce his son's suffering, Guido tells him that this is a game, and they are here to win the grand prize, the tank in the camp's yard. He then makes up the rules: they must endure the pain, the cold, and the hunger, and whoever does this best without complaining will win the prize. In this movie, while everyone else is terrified and immensely suffering, the child is having fun in a concentration camp, only because of a different framing of the experience and the altered understanding he has of it. In chapter 12, I will explain more about how the meaning we create, or is created for our experiences, will affect how they touch our emotions of fear and anxiety.

This movie is also an example that our perception of how dangerous something is may not necessarily accurately reflect the real level of danger. Based on our past experiences, what we are told about the situation, how much we know about it, how prepared we think we are to face it, and the angle we look at it, we can have different degrees of threat assessment. Even the same person may have a different understanding of the same situation, at different times and in different mental and emotional states. Like the case of Guido and his son, sometimes danger is defined for us by others we trust. This is especially true about children who rely on their adults' assessment of danger, because they lack a fully developed cognitive appraisal system, and knowledge they need to draw an informed conclusion.

This also happens in adults. Imagine during an adventure in the Amazon, suddenly your guide tells you that a dangerous snake has been spotted in that area. Without having seen the snake, your state of mind immediately changes to threat screening and detection. Our tendency for learning from others opens the possibility of abuse of fear when leaders of the tribe, whether political or religious, convince their followers that another group of people they barely know are out to get them or their resources. I will discuss abuse of fear in politics in chapter 14.

Uncertainty, Better Safe Than Sorry

Usually, the less we know about something, the easier it is to fear it or over-estimate the risks. For a person who does not know about snakes, it is easy to be afraid of all snakes. But for someone who is educated about different types of snakes, it is easy to spot a nonvenomous one and not be afraid. While it is easy to read and learn about snakes, in more complicated situations it is harder to overcome uncertainty, especially when the information is not available, or contradicting. The recent COVID-19 pandemic is a great example. When it started, we knew very little about the virus, the risk, and its ways of spreading. We did not know much about how to protect ourselves, what masks are better and where to wear them, and if or how much we needed to disinfect the surfaces. As research shed more light on these issues, we gained more confidence and learned where we ought to be cautious and where there was not much risk (e.g., disinfecting groceries). One great way that *knowing* helps is gaining the skills we need to face a potentially dangerous situation and avoid the risks.

Sense of Control

A sense of control, whether real or perceived, helps a lot. Animal research shows that when an animal has a perception of control over the level of pain or suffering, it is less stressed. This is also true about us humans. The less control we have over a situation, the more scared and stressed we are. When the pandemic started, we did not have vaccines or effective medications, or much knowledge on how to protect ourselves. The best we could do was to stay at home. Some became too obsessed with the things they thought they could control and, for example, started to obsessively disinfect all the surfaces in their houses several times a day. This allowed them to feel and exert some level of control over something that was pretty much out of control. A perception that we have some ability to control threatening situations, even if false, helps a lot in controlling our fears. Throughout the history, we have repeatedly tried to find this false sense of control by creating superstitions, myths, and beliefs that if we do certain things in a specific way, we can prevent bad things from happening; for example, if you knock on wood, it prevents bad things from happening to something you hold important and precious. Or if you sacrifice an animal to the Olympian gods, they will keep the flood and the famine away.

A true sense of control, however, not only limits fear, but also is productively helpful in harm reduction. During the pandemic, getting vaccinated or wearing masks played this role for a lot of people, who now more confidently could live their lives knowing they were less likely to acquire severe illness.

Instead of offering sacrifices to Olympian gods, science and engineering have enabled us to build more solid houses resistant to earthquakes.

Transition

Transition, whether positive or negative, is often stressful as it requires readjusting our ways of doing things, learning new skills, and navigating new and less experienced challenges. It also affects our perception, sense of certainty, and control over the new situations. Transition during the pandemic was enormous. When it started, we had to change major aspects of our lives: the way we worked (or many of us lost our jobs), the time we spent with our family vs. our coworkers as we transitioned to remote work, how we vacationed, how and where we worked out, and how we socialized. Overnight we had to become familiar with new technology, and Zoom became a thing that hovered over most of our work and social life. This transition led to a very high level of anxiety and mental illness in society. Based on a report by the Centers for Disease Control and Prevention published in April 2021, during August 2020 through February 2021, the percentage of adults in the United States with recent anxiety or depression increased from 36.4 percent to 41.5 percent.

Proximity

When the threat is distant, or is perceived as distant, we are less afraid and use fewer harm avoidance behaviors. While this makes sense, there is also a loophole: our brains do not seem well equipped to assess the danger of distant or less concrete threats. Overall, physically or temporally distant threats that are outside our own personal experience seem less scary, regardless of how dangerous they may really be when they arrive, or how much preparation we need for when they arrive. Things that happened a hundred years ago (Spanish flu) or might happen a few decades from now (potentially disastrous effects of climate change) do not trigger much fear or action in us. In the case of the recent pandemic, as the tragedy was unraveling in Asia and then in Europe, many Americans and even their leaders did not feel a great sense of urgency to prepare for its landing in the US. We literally treated it as if we were watching the movie *Contagion*. Even when it exploded in New York, many of those living in other states did not take it seriously. We had to see it in our own towns and neighborhoods to be able to understand the urgency of the situation. For some of us, this did not even happen until we lost loved ones to the virus.

Context

Context is a set of circumstances that provide the background information about the physical space, social environment, time, relationship between the items in the environment, and the viewer's relationship to this whole setting. Context is the reason our emotional reaction in proximity to an angry lion in the African Sahara is very different than in the proximity to the same angry lion in a zoo. In the second context, the happy crowd (social context), metal bars separating the lion from us (physical context), and the sign "Zoo" (cognitive context) trigger the emotions of joy and curiosity, although the lion is the same. Especially for us humans, context has a very broad combination of different elements, which include social circumstances, physical space, and time. Time is a fascinating aspect of context that affects our emotions. Many of us start to feel anxious or sad near the anniversary of a bad experience or a loss. Someone who was robbed in a neighborhood in the evening may feel not only nervous near that neighborhood, but also even more anxious in the evening.

Internal context is also important in experience of fear and anxiety. Cognitive context, which is the information and memories kept in our thoughts, is a part of it. For instance, if when you come to work you hear that your boss was angrily looking for you, the cognitive information you will carry for the next minutes and hours until you meet with said boss will increase your anticipatory anxiety. Memories, hormonal state, and the internal emotions we bring to a situation affect experience of fear and anxiety. In the above example, if you came to work already anxious or angry because you heard some bad news in the morning, or had a disagreement with your partner, the anxiety in anticipation of meeting the boss can even be worse.

In chapters 4, 8, and 9 I will explain in more detail the important role that context plays in our experience of fear and anxiety, how it helps us navigate scary situations, and how it can also cause unnecessary fear and anxiety.

Chapter 2

Wired to be Wired

Fear in the Brain

I am not at all in disagreement with you, not at all inclined to leave the psychology hanging in the air without an organic basis. But apart from this I do not know how to go on.

—Sigmund Freud, in a letter to Wilhelm Fliess, September 1898

A curious species, we have always yearned to know or at least imagine the source of our emotions and experiences. Such objective or imaginary insight helps us feel more in control of the panic of "what is happening to me?" While in his time Freud did not have the tools he needed for studying emotions in the brain, we have come a long way in beginning to learn the true origin of our emotions and feelings.

Historically, we have attributed our negative emotions and mental agony to outside forces, gods, nature, animals, spirits and demons, uterus, liver, and bile. We have historically seen the heart as the birthplace of the emotions. Fear and bravery have both been perceived as a work of the heart, and we still use words like bravehearted. It is because we often experience fear in our body, especially in the lower chest and stomach area in the form of tightness or butterflies. Today, we know that although fear is experienced in the body, it starts in the brain. We experience this emotion when the brain areas involved in fear processing create a reaction to an external or internal trigger. Even awareness of the physical sensations related to fear (shortness of breath or chest tightness) takes place in the brain. The bodily reactions and changes that happen when we are scared are the result of neuronal and hormonal commands coming to the body from the brain, triggering a fight, flight, or freezing fear response. Amazingly, the brain tissue itself cannot sense anything, including pain. That is why neurosurgeons can operate on a brain while the patient is awake during the surgery!

I always ask my anxious patients, "Do you feel it more in your head or in your body?" Some of them are more aware of the mental aspects (anxious thoughts, ruminations, worrying, poor concentration), and some experience it more in their body (rapid heartbeat, chest tightness, shortness of breath, tingling of the fingers).

While avoiding science jargon, in this chapter I will explain how fear is processed in the brain. Then in the next chapter, I will walk you through the works of fear in the body, and the physical representations of anxiety and fear.

FEAR PROCESSING BRAIN REGIONS

Many years ago, I was sitting in my parked car when a fast motorcycle hit my car hard on the driver's side. Thankfully no one was injured, although my first brand-new car was damaged badly. I can still recall the detailed memory of the encounter like it was filmed in slow motion, as if time slowed down. I did not see or hear anything other than the approaching bike. This all was because my brain had immediately switched to a totally different mode of operation to enhance my alertness, sense of time, concentration, and memory.

A lot of what we know about our fear brain comes from animal research studies. Because fear is a very primitive mechanism, we share abundantly brain circuits involved in fear processing with animals as primitive as mice and rats. In facts, some of the research on fear, and related mental disorders, still happens in animal research laboratories. In this chapter, though, I will only explain the major brain networks involved in processing of fear. Although there is still a lot to be learned about production and control of fear in the human brain, we have come a long way. It is important to know that although I will talk about each region of the brain separately, these regions do not really function in isolation from each other; there are rather networks functioning in concert. These networks are so closely connected with thousands of feedback loops among themselves that it is almost impossible to see them as separate regions.

While historically, neuroscience research was limited to animal research and postmortem autopsy of the human brain, recent advances in brain imaging techniques have enabled us to see what happens in the brain of a live human. Magnetic resonance imaging, or MRI, is a technique that allows us to study in great details the brain structures. MRI not only shows different parts of the gray and white matter, but also allows us to measure the size and structure of these areas, and learn about the brain changes caused by mental illnesses.

Before we get into details of the brain regions and their interactions, just a quick refresher about brain cells, or neurons: gray matter is a collection of brain cell bodies where the processing takes place, and white matter is mostly made of axons of these cells. An axon is a long extension of the nerve cell and connects one nerve cell to another, or many others. Axons could be seen as the long arms of each nerve cell that taps the other ones on the shoulder and tells them what they should do next. In other words, axons create a network of the neuronal cells that work together. The point of connection between a neuron's axon and the next neuron's body is called the synapse. A very small electrical signal travels through the axon and, when it reaches the end, triggers the release of a chemical, which is called a neurotransmitter (facilitating transmission of the signal from one neuron to the next). After release, the neurotransmitter sits on a receptor on the postsynaptic neuron and activates or inhibits that neuron. Based on the type of neurotransmitter, the neuron releasing and the neuron receiving it, and the type of receptor that grabs the neurotransmitter, this could trigger or suppress activity of the receiving neuron. In summary, gray matter is mostly a collection of billions of neuronal cells, and white matter is the connections between these cells. The lighter color of the white matter is mostly because of the myelin, which covers the axons of the neurons. While gray matter is known to most people as the cortex (the outer layer covering the brain), there are also regions of gray matter deep inside the brain that form several very important areas involved in fear processing.

HOW WE LEARN ABOUT THE LIVING HUMAN BRAIN

The traditional way of looking at the brain was to open the skull after death. These methods have helped us in establishing the foundation of our understanding of the brain anatomy, connections between different parts of the brain, and counting the estimated number of nerve cells in each region. Recent advances in physics and technology have led to building amazing new tools for looking inside the living brain. MRI is a noninvasive imaging method that uses a magnetic field to determine the nature of the molecules in different parts of the brain or body. Simply speaking, MRI charges the molecules with magnetic energy and aligns them in the direction of a strong magnetic field. Then pulses of radio waves disturb the alignment of these molecules. When the pulses stop, each molecule will take a different amount of time to realign with the magnetic field. The energy that is released from these molecules allows the MRI scanner to identify the brain tissue that is made of these molecules. Then the MRI scanner creates a 3D image of the brain with relatively good resolution, showing gray and white matter, and brain subregions.

Functional MRI, or fMRI, is a more novel, complicated, and exciting method that helps us track changes in the blood flow to different brain regions. Like our muscles, brain regions receive more blood when they are more active. By monitoring blood flow, fMRI indirectly tracks what the brain is doing dynamically. For example, we can show a person a scary image, and then see which parts of their brain react first, or most, to seeing this image. Those areas with increased level of activation need a higher supply of blood and oxygen, and fMRI can catch that. This allows us to examine the dynamic function of the brain, and how its networks interact with the outside world and with each other.

Amygdala

The amygdala is the core of the fear processing network in the brain, and essentially where the fear starts. This is an almond-shaped part of the gray matter that sits in the temporal lobe of the brain near our ears. Sensory inputs to the brain enter the amygdala where a decision is made about their emotional relevance or "salience," mostly to basic animal instincts. When we see an object, the amygdala determines if we should eat it, run away from it, attack it, or have sex with it. Threat detection is a critical function of the amygdala, happening in a split second and often at a subconscious level. That means some of the sensory inputs enter the amygdala and trigger unconscious reactions even before these inputs are consciously processed and we have thought about them. This explains our immediate fast reaction to danger even before having thought about it. For instance, if a car or a predator is rapidly approaching us, we first move out of the way or run, and then start feeling the mental and physical presentations of the fear response (e.g., heart pounding), or thinking about who was driving the car, why it was coming toward us so fast, or what was that animal, or if it was just a friend wearing a fluffy costume trying to scare us. Sometimes amygdala responses are so subtle that we may not even be consciously aware of them. For example, if you see a picture of a scared or angry human face while lying in the MRI scanner, we can see increased blood flow to your amygdala. This image normally does not create any conscious emotion in anyone, and you might be too bored in the scanner to even pay attention to it. However, researchers can see an increased activation in the amygdala in response to the image you saw.

As social animals, we are very sensitive to the emotions of other humans, especially their negative emotions. A view of a scared or angry human might mean there is an immediate danger threatening us or our loved ones and the brain and the body need to get ready to respond. Interestingly, research has shown that such responses could be affected by our past experiences. For example, in those with a history of trauma, or childhood exposure to adversity and poverty, the brain may be more reactive to signs of danger. In an fMRI research study, our team found that a brain of an adult who was raised in poverty showed a larger amygdala response to a view of a scared or angry face than the brain of a person who was raised in a middle-income family. We hypothesized that such difference is because the environment of poverty may expose the child's brain to more adverse experiences such as crime, bullying, and less safe neighborhoods. As a result, the developing child brain is trained to be more prepared to respond to tough experiences for self-protection.

The amygdala's role in fear processing is so integral that damage to the amygdala leads to not only absence of a fear response, but also impairment in the ability to learn what to be afraid of. The amygdala is not only involved in starting the fear response, but also the experience of anger, pleasure, sadness, and other emotions. The deep connection between fear and aggression, that I will discuss in chapter 7, has roots in this intimate anatomical and functional connection.

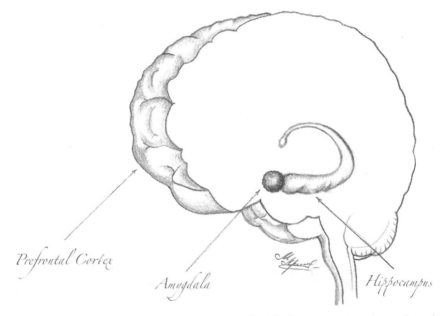

Figure 2.1 A view of the major brain areas involved in fear processing: the prefrontal cortex, the amygdala, and the hippocampus. Courtesy of Maryna Arakcheieva.

When the amygdala determines that we need to take action to fight or avoid danger, it activates other brain areas engaged in preparation and execution of the fight-or-flight responses. Brain regions that process motion and physical actions prepare for planning and execution of motor reactions that we need to fend off or escape the threat. The amygdala also sends signals to the hypothalamus, which in turn activate the sympathetic nervous system, and hormones involved in immune response and bodily functions that need to increase or decrease in a state of crisis. In the next chapter I will explain these bodily responses and the neuronal and hormonal pathways engaged in their working.

The amygdala is vital not only in fear reaction, but also in learning of what we need to be afraid of, or *fear learning*. We are not born with a full understanding of what might be dangerous to us and what might not. As well, there are things that can be dangerous in some situations and not in others. Thus, it is important for us to be able to adapt and adjust to the specific dangers of our environment and learn what is dangerous and should be avoided in a given situation. While we might inherently know an angry human moving fast toward us is not good news, we are not born with a natural inclination to be afraid of a human pointing a gun at us, because gun is a more recent invention of humans. Although we commonly fear snakes, we are not born to be afraid of wolves maybe because our ancestors lived with dogs for a long time. Or it might be more reasonable to be afraid of snakes in the southern states of the US where there are more venomous ones, than, for example, in Michigan, where one can rarely face a venomous snake. The amygdala has a central role in learning fear when we have a difficult, painful, or dangerous experience with something. Because of the ability for forming fear memories, we do not need to be attacked by an angry grizzly bear every single time we go to pet it. Once we are attacked, we learn to avoid all grizzly bears, or for that matter, all colors and sizes of bears for the rest of our life!

In summary, the amygdala plays a key role in production of a fear response to perceived danger, and learning what is dangerous and should be avoided or neutralized in case of a future encounter. Given the amygdala's mostly automatic functions, fear learning is often an automatic process and we do not need to put conscious effort in it the way we do, say, for math. This automatic nature of fear learning is an important aspect of fear-and-anxiety-related mental disorders, when we are afraid of something (e.g., a tiny spider) that we logically know is not dangerous.

Hippocampus

The hippocampus is an important area of the brain that sits in the temporal lobe right next to the amygdala, and is densely connected with it. Most people know it for its role in memory and learning. Learning of fear and safety is also a function of the hippocampus. One fascinating fact about the hippocampus is that it is highly plastic, and every day new cells are born in it. The myth that the brain does not create new cells after childhood is false, and brain areas like the hippocampus constantly create new cells that are used in dynamic cognitive and emotional learning throughout our life. While mental illnesses including fear-and-anxiety-related disorders can lead to shrinkage of the hippocampus and slowing of its growth, a healthy lifestyle, including exercise, can improve its structure and help it grow.

Besides fear and safety learning, the hippocampus is also involved in emotion regulation, and modulates the amygdala's response and fear reactions. This happens via several different mechanisms, one of which is *context processing*: the hippocampus puts things in the context. As I explained in chapter 1, context is a set of circumstances that provides the background information about the physical space, social environment, time, connections between the items in the environment, and the viewer's relationship to this whole setting. When we are at a zoo or a haunted house, context lets us know that the scary object (lion in the zoo, or murderer in the haunted house) is not dangerous. When one hears a loud noise in the context of a combat zone, they immediately drop to the ground for safety. But hearing that loud noise in a shooting range does not warrant such reaction. The amygdala does not see the context and only reacts to the objects. When the lion is seen, the amygdala fires up and is ready to activate the fight-or-flight cascade to keep us safe. Then the hippocampus steps in, sees the context of the zoo, and, through inhibitory axons to the amygdala, tells it to calm down. These negotiations between the amygdala and the hippocampus happen at an automatic and unconscious level; we do not even feel the fear response that was triggered in the amygdala. In the case of the haunted house, we feel it, but we enjoy this sense of excitement.

Animal research has shown that damage to the hippocampus impairs this context processing. After damaging this brain region, the rodent would no longer show the freezing behavior in the physical context that was paired with danger (the cage in which the animal was repeatedly shocked). As I will explain later, in disorders such as posttraumatic stress disorder (PTSD), context processing is impaired, and the hippocampus is smaller and less reactive. When hearing fireworks, the brain of a veteran with PTSD might not differentiate that loud noise from one that happens in the battlefield. As a result, the veteran may experience panic or drop to the ground automatically.

The hippocampus is also involved in learning that something that was previously associated with danger is safe now. For instance, in a person with fear of dogs, even after treatment, the association between the dog and danger is not deleted from the memory. What happens is that the hippocampus separates the dog from danger by forming a new memory. After that, when the person sees a dog, the amygdala may still trigger a fear response, but the hippocampus tells the amygdala that this new dog is safe and blocks the fear reaction. Lack of eradication of the fear memory is a reason that sometimes phobias or PTSD relapse even after successful treatment. That has led scientists to try to find new therapeutics that might be able to erase a fear memory.

Another very interesting function of the hippocampus is *pattern recognition*: it can analyze a perceived pattern and determine what it is. For instance, it breaks a fluffy animal into its different components, and then tries to match each component with the previously recorded memories. The legs may resemble that of a bear or a lion, and the tail could be of a dog or a lion, and the facial fur resembles a lion's mane. The conclusion will be that the observed fluffy creature is a lion. Pattern recognition allows us to not only recognize patterns and objects, but also vague or missing parts of a pattern through the process of *pattern completion*. When a blurry or incomplete object is input to the brain, pattern completion searches in the memories and finds the missing components of the image, determining the full picture. For example, when you read the word "intellgent," you might even not notice that an "i" is missing from the word, as your hippocampus automatically fills in that imperfection. In a later chapter I will touch on how painful past memories can hijack pattern completion and cause misguided perception of danger because of a resemblance of the safe patterns with those that were learned to be dangerous in the past.

Insula

The insula is another part of the gray matter that is located more toward the front of the brain in relation to the amygdala, and is densely connected with it. The insula has a multitude of functions including social empathy and perception of internal sensations or interoception. When we feel our heart beating fast, or chest tightness or stomach upset, the insula is engaged in processing these sensations. The insula also allows us to be aware of our own pain and negative emotions, including fear and anxiety. In other words, when the amygdala triggers a fear reaction, the insula offers a conscious awareness of fear reaction in the mind and the body.

Prefrontal Cortex

This part of the gray matter, which sits right above our eyes and in the forehead, is responsible for many of our complicated conscious brain functions including thinking, decision-making, judgment, and planning. Neuroscientists divide the prefrontal cortex into several subregions based on their different specialized functions, but for ease of understanding, I will refer to the prefrontal areas that are involved in emotion processing as the prefrontal cortex. Like the hippocampus, the prefrontal cortex is involved in context processing and allowing us to understand a potentially dangerous object in the larger picture. Another important function of the prefrontal cortex is the integration of thoughts and instructions in fear processing. For example, we might have read about the colors and shape of the head of venomous snakes. When we see a snake, we refer to those memories and decide if it is venomous or not, and based on that decision, we will be scared or not. When we see that snake, the amygdala fires up, but our cognitive knowledge allows the fear response to flare up if that snake is venomous, and blocks it by suppressing the amygdala if it is not venomous.

Despite its important role in regulation and reduction of fear, the prefrontal cortex can also cause fear! Very often, the instruction that is processed in this brain region leads to experience of fear by informing us of danger. For example, you might be happily walking in your neighborhood when someone tells you that there is a shooter on the loose in that area. Nothing has changed in your vicinity, and you have not seen the shooter, but you will immediately be scared; the instruction and the thoughts related to the assessment of the risk lead to a determination that you are in danger. In this situation the prefrontal brain is not inhibiting a fear response, but activates the fear reactions by exciting the amygdala. As will be discussed in later chapters, many of our more abstract fears and prejudices originate from these mechanisms and engagement of the prefrontal cortex. Existential fears of the modern human, fear of a nuclear war, fear of a pandemic, and irrational forms of learned fear like racism work in this way.

In summary, when in a potentially dangerous situation, the amygdala assesses the level of threat. If the situation is determined as dangerous, then the amygdala sends signals to motor areas of the brain to prepare them for taking physical action, and to the sympathetic nervous system to prepare the body for fight or flight. Activation of the insula makes us aware of our mental and physical experience of fear and anxiety. Direct neuronal pathways from the amygdala to the prefrontal cortex color our thoughts and adjust more complicated decision-making. The hippocampus puts fear into context and allows us to determine how dangerous an object is in the larger picture and circumstances. The hippocampus also engages in formation of fear memories and learning when a previously dangerous situation is not threatening anymore. The prefrontal cortex does the more advanced thinking and planning related to danger, and often inhibits the primitive fear response when the context or information about the situation tell us we are safe. The prefrontal cortex can also trigger fear when we determine danger based on memories, logic, or information that is relayed to us by others.

Fear Chemicals

Chances are high that you have also heard about the role of adrenaline, dopamine, and serotonin in fear and anxiety, and the medications that control anxiety by manipulating these chemicals. These are molecules in the brain, or neurotransmitters, that allow neurons in the brain circuits to communicate with each other. As I explained previously, activation of a single neuron creates an electric current that travels across its axons. But this current cannot be transmitted directly to the next neuron, which is separated from the original neuron by an open *synaptic* space. To transmit the signal to and activate the next neuron, the original neuron releases a molecule, a neurotransmitter, that lands on a *receptor* at the *postsynaptic* neuron. This binding will activate or inhibit that next neuron. There is a multitude of neurotransmitters in the brain, and each of them, depending on the brain region and the type of receptor they land on in each neuron, may activate or deactivate the postsynaptic neuron.

Here I will briefly mention the major neurotransmitters that are at work in fear networks. These neurotransmitters are importantly the target of the major antianxiety medications that are used in psychiatry for treatment of fear-and-anxiety-related disorders.

The fact that each neurotransmitter can have a different effect on a specific receptor on a specific neuron in a specific pathway or part of the brain makes it impossible to identify each one as an activator or suppressor of fear as a general rule. The reader by now knows that our understanding of fear in the brain is through the lens of networks, and not chemicals. But our current medications are not smart enough to target a network, and affect a specific neurotransmitter all over the brain. I will explain how these medications work in chapter 10.

Norepinephrine is one of the main neurotransmitters in the learning and experience of fear, excitement, alertness, and vigilance; being awake; and focusing. It is the neurotransmitter that keeps us awake and alert the nights before an important interview or exam. In the situations of stress and fight or flight, its increased release leads to a state of heightened arousal to allow careful and constant screening for danger. Norepinephrine also shifts our attention toward any sign of danger, and enhances encoding of memories of what is learned to be dangerous.

During experience of fear, norepinephrine increases activation in the amygdala, hippocampus, and prefrontal cortex. Norepinephrine is also a core player in the sympathetic nervous system's fight-or-flight response in the body, which I will discuss in the next chapter.

Dopamine is a close relative of norepinephrine that is engaged in motivation, motor functioning, and thinking. Dopamine secretion especially in the amygdala is increased during stress and anxiety. This neurotransmitter also enhances fear learning.

Both dopamine and norepinephrine are also key in pleasant, exciting, and thrilling experiences, which explains the overlap between fear and excitement, and why we take interest in scary activities as hobbies (horror movies, roller coasters, or haunted houses). I will delve into the fun aspect of fear in chapter 5.

Serotonin is known by most people for its role in depression, and antidepressant medications like fluoxetine (Prozac) that affect it. Serotonin regulates mood, sleep, appetite, sex drive, aggression, and anxiety. Depending on the type of the neurons and specific receptors it touches, serotonin can increase or decrease anxiety, and potentially help in extinction of fear memories. That is why scientists still don't know how exactly antidepressant medications work!

Gamma-aminobutyric acid, or GABA, is spread all over the brain in enormous levels. GABA has an inhibitory effect on neurons and reduces anxiety. Medications such as benzodiazepines like lorazepam, as well as seizure medications, work on the GABA receptors.

Glutamate, on the other hand, is an activating neurotransmitter that is widely spread across the brain. Glutamate plays a role in strengthening fear and trauma memories. Chronic exposure to high levels of this neurotransmitter causes loss of neurons in emotion regulatory areas of the brain such as the hippocampus and the prefrontal cortex. That is why it is studied as a prime suspect in disorders of fear and anxiety.

There are many other molecules involved in fear, but the above are the major players.

Chapter 3

Why Is My Heart Pounding?
Fear in the Body

Sometimes I am sitting there looking very calm, but inside me there is a storm. My body is talking—no, it is screaming. I feel my guts, my heart pounding in my throat, and I keep my hands covered with my sleeves, so people will not see they are soaking wet!

—Anxious patient

Many of us have been there, when the heart is pounding so hard and breathing is so heavy that it is hard to talk, stomach is upset, we feel the chills down the spine, and the hands are sweaty and shaky. When intense enough, some people may even think they are having a heart attack. Although fear is processed and learned in the brain, we experience it in almost all of our body. When scared or anxious, we feel a variety of physical symptoms like muscle tension, chest tightness, rapid heart rate, pounding heart, shortness of breath or heavy breathing, tunnel vision, and tingling and numbness in the extremities. Traditionally "heart" or stomach were viewed as the organs of fear or bravery in different cultures, and we often do feel this emotion inside our chest or stomach. The feeling is so abundant that cowardice or bravery have been culturally and linguistically tied more to the heart than to the brain. This is scientifically viewed as a result of dense sympathetic innervations to the heart and the gastrointestinal system.

In this chapter I will explain how fear and anxiety that originate in the brain activate a series of bodily reactions in almost all organs, including those we are more aware of (pounding heart), and those we are less aware of (hormonal changes and inflammation reactions) to prepare us for fight or flight.

HOW FEAR TRAVELS FROM THE BRAIN TO THE BODY

As we learned in the last chapter, when determination is made in the brain that we are in danger, the amygdala activates a cascade of events in the brain that prepares us for fight-or-flight mode. While the decisions about where the threat is and what should be done about it are made in the brain, it is the body that gets engaged and utilizes its resources to bring these strategies into action. Before we get to the details of these reactions and the bodily changes that prepare us for facing danger, let us imagine what the body would need for ideal performance during a potentially dangerous situation. Keep in mind that we are looking at a body that evolved over millions of years (in other mammals and our own ancestors) to escape or fight other humans, predators, or other competing species, and evade natural dangers, such as flood or a falling tree or rock. In these situations, we need to completely redirect our limited brain and body resources away from all less vital functions, and to the danger of the moment. These limited resources include our brain processing power, attention, energy reserve, blood supply (that needs to be pumped to the vital organs needed for intense physical activity), energy molecules stored in the muscles, and the ability to protect and recover from injuries and fight potential infection in the wounds. Injuries could lead to reduced physical capabilities and blood loss (we have limited amount of that).

When the amygdala, in consultation with the other areas of the brain including the prefrontal cortex and hippocampus, has decided that we *are* in danger, it sends signals to other brain command centers to activate the bodily fear response. Those include networks involved in learning and execution of motor and physical actions covering a range of behaviors from facial expressions (of fear or anger, for example), to physical movements learned during training and previous experiences for fighting or escaping the threat. This prepares not only the muscles in the body, but also the motor processing areas of the brain that will be sending neural signals to activate those muscles.

Another very important player of fear in the body is the sympathetic nervous system. This is the same enormous neural system that causes "adrenaline rush." This system is activated when we are scared, excited, or thrilled, and in general when we need optimal fast physical performance (including during sports competitions). To make this happen, the amygdala sends signals to another vital part of the brain, the hypothalamus, which is located in the center of the brain and behind the frontal lobe. The hypothalamus has a variety of important functions including regulation of metabolism across the body, body temperature, hunger, secretion of a variety of hormones (growth hormone, thyroid hormone, oxytocin, and sex hormones), and finally activation of the sympathetic and parasympathetic nervous systems. Sympathetic and parasympathetic neurons can be seen as the yin and yang of the nervous system. They both have extensive reach to most important organs, and often function opposite to each other in each of these organs. While the sympathetic nervous system readies us to take action in relation to the outside world, the parasympathetic nervous system organizes the internal maintenance and metabolic behaviors such as activities of the gastrointestinal system, bladder, and salivation. These are energy-consuming functions that are not a priority during a life-threatening situation when it is better to direct energy, oxygen, and blood away from them, and to the organs directly needed for saving our life.

SYMPATHETIC NERVOUS SYSTEM

The sympathetic nervous system (SNS) is a widespread network of neurons that expands through most important corners of the body. It is a chain of neurons that runs parallel to the spine on both sides and sends axons to organs vital for fight or flight and any extensive physical activity. These are situations not only of fear and anxiety, but also heightened activity and arousal, including physical exercise, exciting and thrilling activities and competitions. While we experience a pounding heart when scared, we also have it when working out or running, hunting, competing in sports or any other important activity, or just falling in love. This leads to a large overlap between thrilling and frightening experiences. I will talk more about this overlap in chapter 5 when discussing why we love to be scared.

Now let's delve into how SNS activation affects our body. For us humans, the eyes are probably the most important sensory organs because we rely more on our visual inputs than the sense of smell in scanning for and tracing the threat. Increased SNS activity leads to dilation of the pupils in the eyes to assure maximum visual input. At the same time, our far sight is enhanced to allow us to be more visually vigilant for what might be coming at us from a distance. In the mouth, the salivary production reduces as a function of the SNS, hence our dry mouth when we are nervous. From a functional standpoint, it might make sense to not have wet mouth with a slippery grip. Overall, we do not care much about eating and digesting food during fight or flight, therefore no need for much saliva.

SNS activation also aims at increasing production of energy and economizing its use, for our limited resources to be used for functions that are vital to self-preservation. Among these important resources is glucose, which is a major fast fuel for the vital organs, the brain, and the muscles. For this to happen, the liver, which is a major and quick source of production of glucose, increases its manufacturing. On the other hand, the pancreas reduces secretion of insulin, a hormone that removes glucose from the bloodstream and into the liver and fat cells. Reduction of insulin secretion guarantees a sustained level of glucose in the bloodstream in anticipation of increased need for fuel. Like a car needs oxygen to be able to burn gasoline, our cells need oxygen to be able to burn glucose and produce energy. To increase oxygen supplies, airways in the lungs widen, and breathing becomes heavier and faster, leading to an increased flow of oxygen into the bloodstream. This hyperventilation and increased breathing sometimes is experienced in the form of shortness of breath during high levels of fear and anxiety or panic attacks. Organs that are not directly involved in fight or flight, such as the gastrointestinal system (stomach and intestines), lower their activity and consequently their use of glucose. The stomach and intestines reduce their motility and tighten sphincters; digestion slows down.

Glucose and oxygen are delivered to the muscles across the body via the bloodstream in the arteries and capillaries. To increase availability of oxygen and glucose, the heart needs to pump blood faster and with increased pressure. For this, the SNS increases the heart rate and strength of pumping blood with each contraction. The contraction of the heart muscles becomes stronger and tighter. That is why when scared, we often feel our heart pounding in our chest at a faster rate. The vascular system responds by widening the arteries going to muscles, while tightening those going to the less relevant internal organs such as intestines, spleen and kidneys, and the skin. In the skin there is also increased secretion of sweat; as a result, our skin becomes moist and cold.

Fun fact: changes in the secretion of sweat resulting from oscillations of SNS activity are so dynamic and sensitive that we can track sympathetic activity by measuring moisture of the skin. This is actually very easy: we just need to place two electrodes on the skin of the palm of one hand or two adjacent fingers, and relay a small electrical current between the two electrodes. This current is so weak that the person would not even feel it. When skin is moister, because sweat is more conductive to electricity, the current can more easily travel between the two electrodes, leading to measurable increased "skin conductance." This basically is one way lie detectors work. When the person lies, they may be more nervous, leading to increased SNS activation and skin conductance, a change that can be detected by the lie detector machine. In research, we use this technique for measuring sympathetic response to what may be arousing or scary. For example, if someone's amygdala has associated a sound with a loud noise via Pavlovian fear conditioning, when the sound is played, increased SNS activity increases skin conductance response. By placing two wires on the person's fingers and attaching the wires to a tablet, we can see changes in the skin conductance in real time. In my research lab, for example, we use this method to see how people's bodies react to recall of their traumatic memories. When they remember those stressing memories and tell them to us, we can see how their skin conductance increases.

SNS activation also increases our muscles' reflex responsiveness. This helps the muscles to not only respond faster, but also contract more strongly. That is why when scared we are often more easily startled. My neuroscientist colleagues measure this increased startle response by placing two electrodes near the participant's eye, and measuring the extent of the eye blink response to an aversive or scary stimulus.

In summary, fear and anxiety lead to increased SNS activation, which increases glucose and oxygen supply to the vital organs and reduces such supply to organs not necessary for survival. This is a complex, concerted effort of all our physical existence that has evolved over millions of years in us and other species, to increase our chance of survival to the maximum possible level.

While the SNS has extensive reach to majority of the body organs, it also activates hormonal pathways that release molecules in the blood that can also easily reach the cells in our body and create reactions important for fear response and survival. One of the major hormones of this kind is adrenaline, secreted from the adrenal gland.

ADRENAL GLAND

Each adrenal gland sits on top of one of our kidneys, hence the name adrenal (*ren* meaning "kidney" in Latin). Adrenaline, famously known as the hormone of fear and excitement in pop culture, and noradrenaline are two molecules that are released in situations of fear and excitement from the adrenal gland. These two together are also called adrenal catecholamines. These hormones mostly strengthen the above-mentioned functions of the SNS. For example, they increase heart rate and blood pressure; reduce intestine motility; and increase depth and rate of breathing, dilation of the airways, and sweating. Interestingly, catecholamines also reduce our sensitivity to perception of pain. This is important as during fight or flight when there is increased risk of injuries, pain could be a limiting factor to optimal functioning. By temporarily reducing pain perception, we will be less distracted by pain caused by injuries and more able to continue enduring the tough times. You may have noticed this change of pain perception in yourself when injured during a competitive sports activity. You might not feel much pain during the competition and action but then notice it is stronger after you have left the game and are calming down.

Since during fight or flight there is increased chance of injury and bleeding, the body works its best to preserve the vital and limited blood supply by not only moving it away from the skin, but also easing coagulability or formation of blood clots. Coagulation basically is the process of production of a blood clot, which temporarily seals off a damaged blood vessel to stop bleeding, until the blood vessel is repaired later. Increased SNS and adrenal activation facilitates blood coagulation to reduce bleeding caused by potential injuries.

PARASYMPATHETIC NERVOUS SYSTEM AND FREEZING RESPONSE

As mentioned earlier, sympathetic and parasympathetic nervous systems function like the yin and the yang of the body. The SNS is more active during engagement with the outside world when we need to fend off or evade danger, hunt, or engage in intense physical activity. On the other hand, the parasympathetic nervous system (PNS) tends to the internal functions of the body that are not necessary for immediate fight or flight. These functions are more important for maintenance, eating and digestion, and slowing down for recovery. Contrary to the SNS, the PNS causes constriction in the pupils, reduction in the heart rate, dilation of the vessels to the internal organs, and reduction of blood pressure and respiration. In the gastrointestinal system, the PNS organizes food digestion: salivation, increased intestinal motility, and secretion of enzymes that will break down the food for absorption. While the PNS mostly orchestrates the "peacetime" bodily functions, it sometimes plays a role in fear, when the determination is made that the risk is too high to engage or evade, and it is better to not do anything. In such situations the body goes to a freezing response to avoid life-threatening damage from a danger that cannot be avoided or removed. The PNS shuts down the fight-or-flight response causing immobility, reduced muscle tone, and reduced heart rate and blood pressure. A simple clinical example of the freezing response caused by the PNS is a unique phobia: blood, injury, and injection phobia. In this disorder, when the patient is exposed to a view of blood or injury, or receives or anticipates an injection, they faint because of low blood pressure.

FEAR AND THE IMMUNE SYSTEM

The immune system is most known for its role in defending the body against invasive organisms like viruses and bacteria. It includes the white blood cells in the bloodstream, and the molecules that are released during an immune reaction in the blood, from those white blood cells. Some of these molecules, the antibodies, attach to the invading viruses, cells, or particles, and either destroy them, or attract the white blood cells and other molecules to the site to destroy the intruders. The immunity we acquire against infections by vaccination is by way of forming a memory for production of antibodies that are designed to neutralize the specific molecules in the virus or bacteria targeted by the vaccine. Other molecules secreted from the white blood cells, the cytokines, activate or regulate the immune reactions. Cytokines are like the radio signals relayed between different elements of an army that orchestrate their attack on the enemy, and return to the base when the enemy is neutralized. Impairment or false alarm in this system could have a drastic impact on the function of the military in defending a territory. Such malfunctions in the immune system in the body cause excessive inflammation, or destruction of healthy cells in autoimmune diseases like rheumatoid arthritis.

The immune system is an important part of fear response. Our fear system evolved in an environment that was physically harsh, where fight or flight could often lead to physical harm and injury. There was always a chance of damage to natural barriers against bacteria and pathogens (e.g., wounded skin), and a need for preparedness for recovery mechanisms to heal wounds and injuries. This involves mechanisms of fending off germs that invade the body through these wounds, for example, via the claws of a predator. Activation of the hypothalamus and the SNS increases secretion of cytokines that in turn activate an inflammatory reaction. The immune system moves to a state of heightened alertness, ready to neutralize the invading pathogens. Interestingly, cytokines also affect the SNS and the brain areas involved in fear response, including the hippocampus. Abnormal chronic exposure to a hyperactive immune system may cause damage to the brain and organs. As I will explain in chapter 9, inflammation is on the cutting edge of the research of PTSD and anxiety disorders. An abnormal immune response could in some cases be a part of these diseases, causing damage to the brain, cardiovascular system, and other organs.

WHAT CHRONIC ANXIETY AND STRESS DO TO THE BODY

Chronic stress and anxiety, like in anxiety disorders and PTSD, can cause damage to the body and the brain in the long run. It is like flooring the gas pedal of an automobile nonstop. In the body, this puts pressure on the heart, lungs, and vessels, resulting in an increased risk of a variety of diseases. These include heart disease, high blood pressure, diabetes, obesity, pain, autoimmune diseases, and overall reduced perception of health. The detrimental impact of chronic stress on the brain on the other hand, for example, by shrinking the size, and impairing emotion regulatory function of the hippocampus, causes depression and other mental illness. Therefore, contemporary psychiatry and medicine address mental disorders as not only affecting the mind and the brain, but also as bodily disorders, with detrimental impact on physical health. The imaginary boundaries between the brain and the body do not exist anymore; there is one amazingly interconnected system. In future chapters, I will circle back to the physical health risks of anxiety disorders and posttraumatic stress disorder.

To summarize this chapter, when a determination is made in the brain that we should take action against a threat, through the sympathetic nervous system, adrenal gland, and immune system, the body prepares heightened alertness and optimal activity needed for fight or flight. This requires increased production of glucose (fuel), absorption of oxygen, and blood flow to supply glucose and oxygen to the organs vital for survival. These supplies are rerouted from the organs not important for self-defense, to the heart and the muscles. The heart pumps faster and more effectively, blood pressure increases, and the immune system switches to high alert. These prepare the body for fast and strenuous physical activity as well as the possibility of sustaining injury and bleeding. This is how fear affects our mental and physical existence at the organ and cellular level!

Chapter 4

How We Learn Fear, and How We Unlearn It

Fears are educated into us and can, if we wish, be educated out.

—Karl Menninger, American psychiatrist

INNATE VERSUS LEARNED FEAR

One day when I was a kid, I was in my elementary school playground waiting for my parents to pick me up. I was trying to do some acrobatics on the soccer goal horizontal bar. Right then my parents arrived with my aunt. I got distracted and fell on the ground on my back. Initially it felt okay with little pain. My family rushed to me. My dad looked terrified and kept checking to make sure I was okay. Seeing his worried face, I began to cry, as it felt like something dangerous had happened. My aunt said, "Nothing bad happened, you are okay, why are you crying?" To which I answered, pointing at my dad: "He said I should cry!" My dad did not say that, but in my childish way I was trying to explain that I learned from his behavior that I should be scared.

Although some of our fears seem to be inherent and shared by most of us, we are not born to be scared of the majority of the things we learn to be afraid of later. Many of us to some extent share a fear of snakes, death, heights, darkness, or a rapidly approaching object. These potentially dangerous situations have always threatened our ancestors, and may have in some way been encoded into our genetic memory. Whether we want to call them innate or instinctual behaviors, they appear not to be "learned," although learning can strengthen or weaken them. For example, someone who is educated about snakes and tarantulas may not be as afraid of the nonvenomous ones than others would be. This person will be cautious in the presence of a venomous snake, but may happily touch a snake that is known to them as nonvenom-ous. There are different theories about the origin of innate fears, which are mostly studied in animals. One of the older explanations for this form of fear is the Jungian concept of archetypes as universal primitive symbols, images, and behaviors rising from what Carl Jung called the *collective unconscious*.

Scientists argue that innate fear would help with our survival when facing situations that are universally likely dangerous. Martin Seligman's *prepared-ness theory* suggests that humans are inherently prepared to more easily be afraid of specific objects or situations that have been dangerous to our ances-tors. From an evolutionary standpoint, those who were prepared to learn fear of situations with high potential for threat had a better chance of survival compared to others who were not primed to fear these situations as rapidly. For example, those of our ancestors who were primed to dodge a rapidly approaching object survived better the falling rocks, and transferred their genes to their offspring. Those who were cautious approaching the edge of a valley were less likely to fall to the bottom, and were able to make babies and raise them.

But if some of our fears are innate, why aren't all of us afraid of spiders, snakes, and heights? The answer may be in our subtle genetic differences, or different experiences of ancestors depending on the specific circumstances of their environment. Caution around the edges was not as lifesaving to those who lived in flat terrain as it was to those who lived near the mountains. Furthermore, while we all might have the genetic predisposition, this ten-dency might only activate in certain circumstances of interaction between nature and nurture. For example, someone may be more prone to fear spiders than rabbits. Seeing their mother being terrified of spiders, or a scary movie about giant murderous tarantulas during childhood, this person becomes afraid of spiders. But seeing the creepy rabbit in the movie *Donnie Darko* would be less likely to cause a fear of rabbits in the same person.

Scientists have been able to show this innate susceptibility for learning fear. In an interesting study published in 1989, Cook and Mineka showed rhesus monkeys videos of a scared monkey appearing to react to a toy snake or crocodile, or safe objects like flowers or a toy rabbit. After twelve sessions of training, the monkeys became afraid of the crocodile, but not the rabbit! In a study published in 2010, LoBue and DeLoache showed pictures of snakes, frogs, and flowers in pairs to infants eight to fourteen months old. The infants looked more quickly at the snakes than frogs or flowers. Interestingly, those infants showed a similar pattern of response to an angry human face com-pared to a happy human face: they more quickly stared at the angry faces. The same has been found in adults. In a study published in 2001, researchers presented a matrix of images of snakes, spiders, flowers, and mushrooms, and asked participants to find a designated target image in that matrix. In this study, participants were faster in detecting snakes and spiders than they were in detecting flowers and mushrooms. These findings suggest that like other primates, we may be born to react more rapidly to what is more likely dangerous, whether it is a snake or an angry human.

In a constantly evolving environment, an ability to learn what is dangerous is also extremely vital to the survival of a species. There are many situations that our ancestors did not encounter in the past that could take our lives now. A person born a thousand years ago did not even have an idea what a gun is, but a child born in our time needs to know that this object can take their life. In another example, it would be terrible if our ancestors tried to pet a grizzly bear every time they saw it, even though they had already lost a limb to this experimentation.

LEARNING BY EXPERIENCE

One of the most basic and universal ways of learning fear in humans and other animals is via Pavlovian conditioning or associative learning (often called fear conditioning in research). In Ivan Pavlov's famous experiment with dogs, a neutral sensory stimulus (sound of a bell) was repeatedly paired with presence of an inherently pleasant stimulus (food). Pavlov noticed that the sound of the bell allowed dogs' brains to predict presence of food, and prepare for it by a physiological response: salivation.

Associative learning also happens to aversive stimuli. *Fear conditioning* has been extensively studied in animals, and is a dominant theoretical model for fear- and trauma-related mental disorders of phobias and PTSD. In the simplest forms of fear conditioning, a mouse is repeatedly exposed to a neutral stimulus (a sound or smell; conditioned stimulus), paired with an inherently scary stimulus (scent of a cat or an electric shock that would cause a freezing response; unconditioned stimulus). This causes the mouse's brain to link the neutral stimulus to danger. After the learning period, the mouse freezes in response to the conditioned stimulus that is presented alone and without the unconditioned stimulus.

Associative fear learning is also researched in humans. In my research lab we repeatedly showed on a computer screen pictures of a lamp with different light colors to our healthy participants who were wearing headphones. With a specific color of the light—let say blue—they heard a loud, startling noise. After the training period, the participants were able to tell us the blue lamp predicted the loud noise, but the other colors did not. Interestingly, this learning also happens at an automatic and unconscious level, which was observed in their automatic body response. When they saw the blue light, their body showed an increased sympathetic response, which was visible in their increased skin conductance galvanic response (see chapter 3). Amazingly, fear conditioning can even happen when we are not consciously aware of it! For example, scientists have paired images that were masked by another image (and not consciously seen by the participants) with an electric shock to the hand. Without knowing what happened, the participants' bodies still showed an increased skin conductance response to those masked images! In the clinic we often see this in the form of automatic and unconscious fear and anxiety, of which source the patient cannot identify. A work of psychoanalysis is helping uncover such primitive fear learnings and bringing them to the light of patients' consciousness (see chapter 10).

Fear learning not only happens to the blue lamp, but also to more complicated situations. Researchers have paired sounds or voices, pictures of faces, or even physical contexts with fear. A fascinating aspect of fear conditioning is semantic and conceptual fear learning. A word, a thought, a relationship, a movie, or a social context could coincide with a painful experience. Someone with painful experiences with a tough math teacher may experience anxiety when calculating numbers even years later. If someone was raised by a very critical parent, this person's brain may associate any parental or authority figure with pain and fear. Even as an adult, when interacting with a superior or an authority, this person may panic automatically, without even knowing why they are scared, resulting in fight-or-flight reactions (looking nervous, avoidant, hostile, or oppositional). This in turn would cause negative reactions from the other person, which in the person's mind would confirm their fear. Such a person will always find authorities and managers hostile and uncaring. The Freudian concept of *repetition compulsion*, or a tendency to repeat the same painful interactions with others, could be in part due to these dynamics.

FEAR GENERALIZATION

In my career as a trauma expert, I have worked with many veterans, first responders, refugees, and civilians with PTSD caused by shootings or explosions. There is one day of the year many of these people dread: the Fourth of July! That is because of the fireworks that cause anxiety, flashbacks, and panic attacks in them. I have even had veterans tell me that when they hear the fireworks, they automatically drop to the floor in a defensive position.

This is because of an important aspect of fear learning: *fear generalization*. Fear generalization is the ability to expand a fear response to situations that have some resemblance with the dangerous situation. For example, if a child is attacked by a German shepherd, they may become phobic of all German shepherds, all large dogs, all dogs, or all fluffy animals. Although being afraid of the neighbor's friendly Shih Tzu seems illogical, fear generalization has an evolutionary purpose. Fifty thousand years ago, if our ancestors were attacked by a big brown fluffy animal (brown bear), it made sense to also avoid similar-looking black animals (black bear). It would be an evolutionary disadvantage to try to pet a black bear, a year after having been mauled by a brown bear! The degree of fear generalization depends on a person's genetic predisposition to fear and anxiety, previous experiences, and the severity of the danger or harm in the initial encounter. While my research participants could probably forget in a few days that the blue light was paired with the loud noise, a survivor of a shark attack would definitely not forget that sharks could be really dangerous. Interestingly, fear generalization seems to be greater in children, suggesting that they are more likely to expand fear to what is partially relevant to the feared situation. This may be because this is a critical developmental phase when they are creating an understanding of the world around them, and importantly what could be potentially threatening to them and their offspring.

Fear generalization has been extensively researched in humans. Scientists have shown it in response to shapes relevant to the conditioned stimulus, similar-looking human faces, or even semantically relevant words. For example, fear learning to the term "spiderweb" can lead to a fear response to the term "wasp nest." These forms of fear generalization have important clinical implications, as clinicians try to help patients understand and disentangle how past painful experiences affect their current life. When teaching my students, I often use the following example: imagine someone survives a severe car accident after being hit by a yellow car driven by a young man near a grocery store. This person's brain may associate different aspects of this experience with danger: car, driving, man, young, yellow, grocery store. Based on the unlimited combinations of these different aspects, they can become afraid of driving, yellow vehicles, young drivers, male drivers, or driving to a grocery store, or be nervous anytime they're near any location of that specific grocery store chain.

In treatments like psychoanalysis and cognitive therapy, we try to decipher how past negative emotional experiences can form a person's current emotional reactions, often at an unconscious level. I recall that I had a patient, Mary, a very bright and successful middle-aged professional, who always ended up drinking too much when going out with friends, to the point of embarrassing herself. Although she hated this pattern, she could not stop it, and did not know what led to it happening every time she went out. Upon more exploration during treatment, she noticed an automatic thought: "I am more loved and more interesting to others when I am drunk." We kept digging deeper and she remembered a childhood memory: She grew up in an unhappy home with an absent dad and a depressed mother. But there was a couple in the neighborhood, the Smiths, who were very loving, caring, and kind to her.

She felt that that couple were the only people who paid attention to her. The Smiths, however, were alcoholics and always drunk, and she smelled alcohol when she visited them. We realized that Mary had automatically associated alcohol, its smell, and drunkenness to being loved and appreciated, without consciously being aware of this association.

LEARNING BY OBSERVING OTHERS

As a social species, we learn a lot by observing other humans and our tribe-mates. This evolutionary advantage has served us very well and has allowed us to accumulate knowledge, culture, and skills. Enormous progress in science, learning from history (in which we often fail), and advances in technology and engineering are a result of this cumulative knowledge. Imagine where human civilization would be today if each of us had to learn making fires and inventing the wheel on our own. In schools and colleges, we learn what has been achieved since the beginning of recorded history, via listening to and observing others. We also learn most of our social and personal skills from our parents and caregivers.

We similarly learn a lot of what we are scared of, from other humans. This has tremendously increased our chances of survival as a social animal: fifty thousand years ago, if we saw that a predator injured or killed a tribemate, we all learned to avoid that animal even if we were not attacked by it personally. It would be a disaster if each tribe member had to lose a limb to the predator, to learn via associative learning. We not only learn what to be afraid of from the experience of our tribemates, but also learn what to do to survive. We watched our tribemates fight the enemy, the predators, and natural disasters, and learned their skills. Actually, observing is one of the best ways we learn anything. We still do that: we learn from our parents, peers, teachers, movies, what to be afraid of. They do not necessarily need to tell us that something is scary. We saw that our mom was terrified of spiders, and figured spiders are dangerous. We watched a movie about murderous giant tarantulas, and some of us became afraid of these eight-legged creatures. I have seen many patients with fear of dogs, who came from cultures less close with dogs, or where there were many stray dogs out there. They learned from their parents' faces that dogs are dangerous, or saw that people were attacked by stray dogs. Although they now logically know that their friend's dog is very friendly, part of them does not allow them to get close to it. Some of us do not even remember how and when we learned these fears, but we did.

Learning fear from parents is also seen in other animals. My friend and colleague at the University of Michigan, Dr. Jacek Debiec, did an interesting experiment on rats: before pregnancy, he fear conditioned adult female rats to the scent of peppermint. This was done by repeatedly presenting the scent along with a mild electric shock to their feet. Via Pavlovian conditioning, these rats developed a fear response to the peppermint scent alone. After pregnancy and delivery, the mother rats were presented with the peppermint scent in presence of their pups. Later, the pups (who had never received the shock) showed avoidance fear behavior to the same peppermint scent! This observation is replicated in adult rats, who similarly learn from each other to be afraid of a smell or a sound, without having experienced the shock themselves.

There are similar studies done in humans. Olsson and Phelps had their research participants watch a video of another person going through fear conditioning. The *observed* person received a mild uncomfortable shock to their finger when they saw the conditioned stimulus (e.g., a blue rectangle). After this, the observing participants were told they would be going through the same experiment, but they never received a shock to their finger. However, they still showed a fear response reflected in their skin conductance galvanic response to the blue rectangle.

During rough times like war and natural disasters, learning from parents and caregivers is specifically critical for a child's survival. In a study funded by the National Institute of Child Health and Human Development (NICHD), we have been researching the impact of war trauma and forced migration on Syrian and Iraqi refugee children resettled in the US (I will talk more about this work in later chapters). In this research at STARC, we found a direct connection between refugee children's anxiety level, and severity of symptoms of PTSD and anxiety in their parents: the more anxious and stressed the parents, the more anxious the children. As children do not have a fully developed knowledge base to appraise risks of the outside world on their own, they rely on their parents' assessment. This is a fascinating area of child development, especially in modern-life situations that are less straightforward. For example, how scary should failing an exam or a negative review from a supervisor be? Logically, none of these situations are life threatening or dangerous. But some of us are terrified of them. Through experience, we learn from our parents' reaction to our failures how bad they are. If a person's dad was too disappointed, stressed, or angry when they got low grades in elementary school, they might have learned that failing is really scary. And this learning carries over to their adult life when they can be too worried about any form of social, career, or academic failure.

Transmission of fear and anxiety to future generations is not limited to learning by observation. Children and even grandchildren of people who have survived horrible traumatic experiences, such as the Holocaust, often tend to be more anxious, especially in response to what was threatening to their parents or grandparents. This *intergenerational transmission of trauma* happens not only via learned behavior passed on to future generations, but also via changes in the genes. These *epigenetic* changes can be passed on to children who are born even after parents left the trauma environment, and cause fear and anxiety at a level beyond what is learned from behavior or words of the parents. But what is an epigenetic change? We receive half of our genes (DNA) from our mother and the other half from our father. Genes are codes that, when expressed, orchestrate production of different molecules in our brain and body that define our physical form and behavioral tendencies. Most of these genes are covered by a molecule (are methylated), which turns them off and prevents their expression. When that methylation cap is removed, the gene finds a chance for expression. Epigenetic changes caused by trauma lead to removal or addition of these caps to specific genes, which can be transmitted to the offspring, leading to increased expression of fear-related molecules and consequently behaviors. Although intergenerational transfer of trauma addresses the most extreme situations like the Holocaust, many people inherit some degrees of anxious behavior from their ancestors.

While social learning is an evolutionary advantage, it can also lead to unnecessary fears. First, the fears we learn from our parents or tribemates might have been justified in the past, but not relevant to our time. For example, during war and famine, worrying about safety and food are lifesaving, but the same worries do not apply in the safe civilian life. Children of people who have survived war or famine may show food insecurity or be too cautious, causing health problems, unnecessary stress, or loss of opportunities. Furthermore, our parents and grandparents were not always right in their assessment of danger, even in their time. A parent for whatever reason may have learned that authorities can be dangerous. In anticipation of meeting their boss, this parent might look too anxious and concerned. As a result, their child may grow up with an unnecessary fear of authorities. If a mother is afraid of dogs for a variety of reasons (cultural, personal experience, or learning from others), their child will learn to be afraid of dogs without even knowing how they gained it. In clinical practice, I often help my patients become aware of such fears they learned in the past that are outdated and not useful anymore.

LEARNING FROM WORDS

As a species with highly developed language skills, we learn many of our skills from others' words, whether spoken or written. We also learn what to be afraid of from what others tell us, which is an evolutionary advantage. Thousands of years ago, if the tribe elders advised us to avoid a part of the territory because of predators that lived there, we would listen to them. The larger the told threat, the more likely we would heed the warnings. If it was killer bees, our curiosity could potentially override the warning. But if we were told that grizzly bears have killed several tribe members in that area, we would probably not risk it.

Instructed fear learning, or learning fear from others' words, and its interaction with innate fears, is a fascinating field of research. In a study published in 2018, participants saw fear relevant (spider or snake) and fear irrelevant (butterfly or bird) pictures. They were told that when seeing one picture from each group (e.g., snake and bird), they would receive an unpleasant electric shock in their finger. Then they were shown a "safe" picture on one side of the screen (spider or butterfly), and picture of the bird or the snake on the other side. The shock was, however, never administered. Researchers found that the participants looked faster at the picture that they were told would be followed by the shock (snake or bird). This was regardless of the potential innate fear relatedness of the picture (snake or spider). In a study conducted in my lab, we showed our participants two images (pictures of lamps of different colors). Before the experiment, we told the participants that one of these lamps (e.g., the blue lamp) would be paired with a loud noise played in their headphones. We did not tell them anything about the other (green) lamp. Although they heard the same loud noise after both the blue and the green lamps, they showed a larger galvanic fear response to the blue lamp. Interestingly, when pairing with the loud noise stopped, the participants learned later than normal that the blue lamp was not dangerous anymore! In other words, they forgot the association between the blue lamp and pain more slowly.

In a very interesting experiment, researchers studied the three methods of learning fear that I have explained. Three groups of participants personally experienced, or observed, or were told of pairing of a shock with one image. All three groups learned the association between the image and the shock. Then the researchers masked the original image by immediately showing another picture. Because of that, although the brain networks did process the image, the participants were not "aware" that they saw it. Those who learned fear via personal experience or observing others showed an increased skin conductance response to the image. Interestingly, those who learned it via instruction failed to show the automatic fear response! This means that the fear we learn by instruction or reading only works when we are consciously aware of the presence of the feared object or situation. On the other hand, fears learned by experience, or by observing others, may have deeper mechanisms, be more automatic, and therefore harder to control by logic or calming words.

The fear that we learn from words has taken a complex and abstract form in modern life. In 2020 we learned to be afraid of an invisible organism that spreads in the air (the coronavirus), although many of us did not see it, or anyone who died from it! We were even willing to lose some of our social privileges to avoid a potentially deadly infection. We listen to the authorities when we are told there is risk of a terrorist attack, pandemic, or natural disaster. Advances in communication technologies and media have provided us with effective access to information about these threats, and ways to protect ourselves against the harm. However, learning fear from words of others has its own flaws, and has often led to large-scale catastrophes. We learn from parents, society, and culture things that are not necessarily true. Superstitions like believing in the evil of the number thirteen, or knocking on wood for luck, are more benign forms of these unfounded fears. But trusting the "elders" of the tribe, religion, party, or the country has caused horrible disasters. Leaders have used this biological loophole over and over as an opportunity to dominate people and convince them that their survival depends on the annihilation of others. Racism, nationalism, wars, and genocides are consequences that I will discuss further in chapters 14 and 15.

HOW WE LEARN SAFETY

Learning that something is not dangerous anymore is as important as learning what is potentially dangerous. What is dangerous in one context might not be necessarily unsafe in another. An angry lion is dangerous in the Sahara, but not in the zoo. It is not a great idea to try to pet a wolf in the woods, but domestic dogs are great guardians. In an ever-changing world, adaptation and ongoing learning, including that of fear and safety, is crucial for our optimal functioning and survival.

Mechanisms of learning safety are similar to that of learning fear: personal experience, social observation, and verbal messages. Learning by experience happens through *extinction learning*, a universal mechanism among humans and other animals. We previously learned that in Pavlovian fear conditioning, by repeated exposure, a rat learns to associate a sound with being shocked. After that, playing the sound over and over without pairing with the loud shock teaches the rat that the sound does not predict danger anymore, and stops the fear behavior. Gradual exposure to a safe and friendly dog can teach a phobic person's brain that dogs are not scary. My 120-pound Great Pyrenees Jasper used to help people overcome their fear of dogs by allowing them to gradually approach this gentle giant. Safety learning in a person afraid of dogs can also occur by observing other humans being fine near Jasper. That is the important role the therapist plays in therapy, signaling safety of the situation by the therapist's calm and confident presence. By the way, if you google "the most famous dog in Ann Arbor," you will find an article about late Jasper (12/27/2012–11/28/2021), who was a beloved icon in Ann Arbor, Michigan.

Finally, we learn safety through words. You might be about to scream after seeing a boa, when your friend tells you that it is their pet snake! Leaders and media outlets are powerful sources that can play a role in calming and assuaging the anxieties of societies during the times of stress. Sadly, in our time they often do the opposite, which I will address in the last two chapters of this book.

Pavlovian extinction learning is central to learning that something once perceived as a threat is not dangerous anymore. Although after extinction learning fear memories cease to work, it does not necessarily mean that they are gone. Fascinating recent research shows that fear memories are not erased after extinction (there is still memory of "dog danger" encoded in the brain). What happens after extinction is formation of a competing safety memory. When the previously feared object is encountered, the hippocampus and prefrontal cortex utilize this safety memory to inhibit a fear response in the amygdala. In our research at STARC, we have also found that extinction does not work equally well in all people. After seeing the blue light repeatedly without hearing the loud noise, some of our participants still thought the loud noise would follow the blue light. In fMRI scans of these people, we found a lower activation in the prefrontal cortex, hippocampus, and amygdala compared to others. Interestingly, more anxious people were less likely to extinguish fear as well as those with less anxiety. As I will explain later, abnormalities in safety learning are central in some anxiety disorders and PTSD.

Chapter 5

Haunt My Nerves

Why We Love to be Scared

Horror is a universal language; we're all afraid. We're born afraid, we're all afraid of things: death, disfigurement, loss of a loved one. Everything that I'm afraid of, you're afraid of and vice versa. So everybody feels fear and suspense. We were little kids once and so it's taking that basic human condition and emotion and just f*cking with it and playing with it. You can invent new horrors.

—John Carpenter, American filmmaker, writer, and director of the *Halloween* movies

Since the first time I looked down from the top of a ladder in my childhood, I have always been afraid of heights to some degree. Although I am not phobic, I still feel tingling and weakness in my knees when I watch down the window or stairs of a tall building. But I, the same person, love mountains, have ridden a mule down to the bottom of the Grand Canyon, and have flown in a fighter jet at 450 miles per hour doing loops and barrel rolls.

Humans are complex and at times paradoxical beings. Although fear is one of our most disturbing and actively avoided emotions, we also often actively seek fear. We go out on a limb to avoid danger, seek professional help from a mental health professional, or even use drugs and alcohol to battle excessive fear and anxiety. But at the same time, we frequently seek or fantasize about fear in our myths, folklore stories, movies, and recreational activities.

It is probably impossible to find a culture that does not have stories, legends, fictional characters, or traditions colored by fear. Whether it is Baba Yaga in Slavic folktales, Witch Holda in "Hansel and Gretel," or Zahhak the Snake Shoulder in Persian Iranian myth, people of all cultures have created and enjoyed sharing scary stories. The fear industry is a very successful business, and horror movies are very popular. The movie *It* alone made over

$700 million in gross income since its release in 2017. This means millions of people paid money and spent their leisure time to watch a serial killer demon terrorize some small-town children.

In the United States, an entire holiday is dedicated to fear, as there exist many fear-themed festivals and cultural activities across the globe. Halloween is celebrated globally by people, most of whom do not know its origin, and it is a multibillion-dollar business in the US alone. We all have gone to—or at least contemplated going to—a haunted house. Thrill-seeking recreational activities like bungee jumping and skydiving are popular, and people love to watch others defeat fear, whether by racing in superfast cars or walking a tightrope across the Grand Canyon. But there are also people who do not enjoy horror movies and haunted houses. Some find them intolerably scary, and some find them boring, uninteresting, or childish.

But why do some of us seek an emotional reaction we are biologically wired to avoid and dislike? Why do both anxiety-relieving medications and horror movies have billion-dollar markets? Why do some of us enjoy scary and thrilling experiences, some avoid them, and some are indifferent about them? In this chapter we will explore the human desire for fear as entertainment from both biological and psychological standpoints.

FEAR IN THE FOLKTALES

We color our stories with fear for the same reasons we do romance and violence. These are universal, fundamental, basic, and primal instincts, drives, and emotions that have helped our species survive and procreate. We all experience fear, anger, love, and sadness, and are highly programmed to detect and relate to these emotions in others. Regardless of the pleasant or unpleasant nature of these emotions, they help us make intimate bonds with others, and with ourselves.

As humans, we tend to project ourselves, our thoughts, feelings, and internal experiences onto the outside world. We see the world in our own image, and attribute our own thoughts and emotions to our environment. It does not surprise us when a tree talks; a dog walks on two legs in a movie; or when Zeus, creator of the universe, is portrayed as a bearded old man. We also do this every night in our dreams. Most of us have fallen prey to predators or demons or have been chased by a dangerous enemy while sleeping. Our unconscious brain processes its fears, wishes, frustrations, and ambitions in a symbolic way, and in the form of scenarios created by "actors" picked from our memories. A modern American may have a terrible nightmare about being shot at, and a medieval Japanese person dream of being killed by a katana sword. We also reflect our deeper, older fears in our dreams.

In psychoanalytic theory, a man who is afraid of women because of painful early experiences with his mother may have nightmares of encountering scary witches in his basement. I had a police officer who lost a colleague in a shooting frequently wake up from nightmares of being chased or shot at. In therapy, we use dreams to learn about deep fears and unconscious wishes and conflicts of our patients. In Freud's view, dreams are *the royal road to the unconscious.*

Nations and cultures also dream in the form of myths and legends that reflect the collective desires and fears of a people. Most of these fears and wishes are universal regardless of time and geography. Like we all, regardless of culture or nationality, have dreams of flying, falling, or being chased, nations separated by geographical distance or time have created very similar myths with imaginary creatures like dragons, demons, wizards, and witches. We do not necessarily "enjoy" a scary dream or myth, but we relate to it, as it is part of us. We are absorbed by it because it intimately resonates with our innermost mental operations. It speaks to the primitive human inside. Carl Jung has used the term *collective unconscious*, an ancestral unconscious memory and shared functioning of humankind, to describe this phenomenon.

When we are anxious, worried, scared, or stressed by something, we more often have scary dreams. Similarly, in times of threat and uncertainty, nations may produce and consume more fear-colored tales, myths, or movies.

BIOLOGY

In the previous chapters we discussed that the amygdala; the sympathetic nervous system; and the neurotransmitters dopamine, epinephrine, and norepinephrine are main players in experience of fear. Interestingly, there is a major biological overlap between fear and excitement. The amygdala, sympathetic nervous system, and the same neurotransmitters are also engaged during positive thrilling experiences. We even use the term *adrenaline rush* to describe the experience of thrill in part due to increased adrenergic activation. Dopamine and norepinephrine are involved in processing both thrilling excitement and fear. Bodily experiences of falling in love, intense competitive sports, exciting video games, and anxiety also largely overlap. During all these situations breathing is heavy, the heart beats faster, attention is focused, and we feel overly awake and alert. The fight-or-flight system is also the thrill and excitement system. Many exciting activities, such as professional sports, also require the level of high-intensity performance that is activated during fight-or-flight situations.

By throwing ourselves into scary but safe experiences, we trigger the same physical and mental reactions. We startle the animal within, to enjoy the fast ride, knowing that we are safe and there is no real danger. For this to work, it is required that we know we are safe, to allow the prefrontal brain and hippocampus to step in for a controlled fear response in the amygdala. To some extent it is like when your dog sees a wolf on the TV: he does not know the difference between a real wolf and the one on the TV and gets riled up. But you know the difference, and curiously watch your dog's reaction.

The difference between us watching a horror movie and the dog watching TV is our ability to put the scary experience in context. We know the murderer is in the TV and not in our living room. Being chased by a masked person with a knife will be a very different experience based on if it happens in a dark alley or a dark haunted house. Although the amygdala is fired up in both cases, the contextual brain controls this reaction and allows us to enjoy the haunted house scene.

THE BALANCE

For any thrilling experience to be enjoyed, there needs to be a proper balance between the fear response triggered in the lower brain, and the sense of safety and control in the logical frontal cortex. In other words, the situation must have an *optimal level of subjective realism* and be believable enough, but not too believable. In this case, part of us dissociates from reality and is absorbed in the horror movie, but in the background of our mind we know we are safely sitting on our own couch with a glass of wine and pizza. As different minds might differ in balancing the believable and the fake, some could enjoy a movie, some may find it too scary, and some may get bored and find it stupid. Even the same person may find one scary movie exciting, another boring, and a third one hard to watch. The ability to dissociate from reality and be absorbed in the experience is also very important for such experiences. Dissociation from reality helps us disconnect from our usual life and its distractions, join the characters in the movie, and two hours later find ourselves back on our couch.

When the thrilling experience feels too real, when there is a sense of loss of control or a lack of trust in our safety, it may become intolerable. In all these cases, the logical brain cannot keep the fear response within the optimal window, and fear gets out of control. It is like a terrified dog pulling the leash so hard that you cannot control it anymore. Even in the same person, different scary experiences may have different outcomes based on their perception of the realism. I find *Nightmare on Elm Street* an entertaining horror movie because the context and characters do not feel too real to me and I could not imagine it happening in my life. But the first time I saw the movies *The Exorcist* and *Hereditary*, I got a good scare. When I saw *The Exorcist* in my teenage years, the story felt too real, and possible to happen in my own bedroom. That night, only teenage pride stopped me from asking to sleep in my parents' bedroom!

When the unrealness of the experience is too obvious, or when the objective analytical thinking is too involved, it will steal the excitement out of the experience. I recall the first time I was watching *The Walking Dead* zombie series with a friend. Being a physician, I was too analytical about the human physiology in the zombies. I thought it was impossible for a zombie to walk without a living heart pumping blood and sending oxygen to their muscles. How could those muscles work without the fuel they need for their performance? I kept talking until my physician friend said, "If you really want to enjoy this movie, you have to shut down your analytical brain." The advice worked.

A sense of control, and certainty and trust that we are safe are also at work during a thrilling scary experience. If someone loses the sense of control over the situation, or is too unfamiliar with the experience, they may find it hard to tolerate. We know that we can turn off the TV or pause the horror movie whenever it gets too scary and we need a break. Imagine watching the scariest movie you know, alone and without the ability to turn it off or pause it. Similarly, what stops many people from riding roller coasters is that when it starts, there is no way to get off it before the full ride ends; there is no pause button. The degree of this sense of control plays a very important role in what each person finds optimally exciting and what is too much for them.

The control we have during watching a horror movie or being at a haunted house contrasts with many worrying realities of life that we cannot control. This sometimes is the reason that people take refuge in unrealistic scary thrills to compensate for those uncontrollable real-life experiences. Many thrill seekers actually do experience a lot of anxiety in real life. The skydiving or bungee jumping gives them an opportunity to be in a scary or worrying situation that they can manage. They achieve the control they lack in real life, by exposing themselves to a controllable scary situation.

Trusting the system, or others who are in charge of our safety, is another contributor to the joy of the thrill. If you trust that the actors at the haunted house are not allowed to touch you, you may feel less scared compared to when they might touch you. At the amusement park, someone who knows the science and engineering used in the making of the roller coasters can trust their safety more than someone who heard rumors that people have died because of malfunctioning of the machines.

PRACTICE

When I was a child, one night I was watching a documentary about lions with my father. The lion cubs were playfully wrestling with each other and nipping at their mother. My dad asked me, "Arash, why do you think the cubs are doing this?" I answered, "They are just playing." "They are not just playing," he said, "they are also practicing and rehearsing fighting and hunting for when they grow up." He was right. By biting, wrestling, and chasing each other, the cubs were practicing the skills they would need for future battles and hunts. The safety of their mother's guardianship was a great opportunity to learn the skills for when they would be on their own.

But could this also apply to us humans when we volunteer for scary situations? Could we be mentally or physically practicing how to survive dangerous situations, in a safe context? This makes more sense when we are reminded that we evolved in much harsher environments centuries, thousands, and hundreds of thousands of years ago. We and our tribemates were frequently threatened by dangerous encounters, whether a predator, a natural disaster, or another tribe. Through these experiences we naturally learned how to problem solve and stay safe in danger. We also learned from the experience of our tribemates, for example, by listening to stories of the elders about their fights and hunts. It is quite possible that a function of our tendency for thrilling experiences, movies, and stories is to practice alertness, readiness, and problem solving by watching the things that help the movie or myth characters survive or cost them dearly. This is not much different than our ancestors listening to their shaman narrating an exciting and yet scary story of a hero saving the tribe from witches and demons. This allows us to practice, in our minds, ways of escaping or neutralizing danger. How many times have you found yourself yelling at the movie characters what they needed to do to be safe, or even got angry and disappointed that they did not take your advice? Have you caught yourself problem solving in your head and imagining what you would do in the unsafe condition of the movie actors? We also learn from the skilled-in-survival characters how to save our lives if this were to happen to us. People were excited to see how Daryl and Carol skillfully navigated the atrocious situations that killed others in *The Walking Dead*. We seem to use these opportunities to update and advance our defenses, and to prepare for when real danger might happen. Like the lion cubs, we may not even be aware that we are practicing, but nature knows what these instincts are doing in us.

The thrilling experiences often end with a sense of achievement and pride, a sense of control, that we did it and survived. We reward ourselves for survival; we now are the hero who is still alive after other people in the movie were killed by the mysterious creatures. We are the one among our friends who had the courage to get on the scariest ride at the park, or to go to the scariest part of the haunted house. To the primitive part of us, the victory is even more real, like the dog that scared away the wolf on the TV.

A MINDFUL EXPERIENCE

Fear is one of our most consuming emotions. It easily kidnaps all our senses and absorbs all our attention away from anything and everything else. To survive danger, we completely dedicate all our psychic performance to the feared situation, and away from anything else that is not important for survival at the moment. Fear makes us forget everything else. That makes it a very mindful emotion that anchors us in the here and now, away from thoughts of the past and the worries of the future. When watching a horror movie, we rarely think about the disagreement we had with our boss earlier in the day, or the exam that is coming up next week, or the contractor who has really frustrated us with their terrible service. The same way mindfulness practices bring us to the here and now and away from our frustrations, worries, and ruminations, a horror movie or skydiving totally distract us from those other real-life fears and worries, and bring us to the very moment we are in. In fact, mindfulness is one of the best methods for dealing with anxiety, daily worries, and sad thoughts—and is highly recommended by mental health professionals.

A BONDING OPPORTUNITY

We rarely engage in entertaining scary and thrilling things alone. While we regularly watch movies, shows, and documentaries alone, we tend to watch scary movies or go to haunted houses or amusement parks with friends and family. Besides increasing the sense of control as a group, being with others allows us to share the heightened emotional experience. High emotions often enhance bonding and tighten our relationships. We share a good scream, laughter, or a sigh of relief at the haunted house. We also brainstorm and share thoughts about what the movie characters should do to stay safe, and learn from each other how to be alert for the next haunted house actor jumping at us. These shared experiences allow for a deeper tribal bonding and sharing of our solutions, defenses, and skills. We also share the bonding and comradery experiences of a tribe surviving a dangerous situation together.

WE MIGHT NEED IT

When I was younger, I was afraid of heights to the point that I could not climb a ladder to the attic. One year a friend suggested that I spend my vacation in the Grand Canyon. Also at her recommendation, I signed up for a mule ride down the canyon. I did not have a clear idea of what I had gotten myself into until I arrived at the place. This was *not* a good idea for a someone afraid of heights, but it was too late to change my mind. I would be very embarrassed if I backed out in front all these other people. The walls stood straight, and I could see the bottom of the canyon; the trails were steep and iced. The mules loved to walk on the edges, as they were very skilled and confident in what they did. We were told that during decades of this ride, no mule or person had fallen down the canyon. When they made a U-turn, I could see a few thousand feet below! The December icy trail did not make it easier as at times they would slip on the ice. At the end of this scary ride, and over the next few days, I had an interesting observation: I was much less stressed and anxious than usual.

This and other experiences have led me to think we might need some regular exposure to a healthy dose of real fear in our lives. Our modern life is too safe compared to the environment in which our fear system evolved. In our time, our fear circuitry does not get enough "exercise." We know that we need to exercise our muscles, heart, and lungs because they evolved in situations of frequent intense physical activity. We feel happier and less stressed when we regularly exercise, because our bodies did not evolve to sit at a desk all day. We go to the gym to give our body the kind of physical task it was meant to do on a regular basis. The same might also apply to our fear system. Today we live in an extremely safe environment, and most of our modern-life fears and anxieties are irrelevant to the way our fear system evolved. Some of them may even be due to a lack of normal exposure to what should be scary. We may be exercising our fear system by safely entertaining scary and thrilling experiences, the same way we exercise our body. Exposure to the fears that resonate with our evolution may also put fears and anxieties of modern life into context and rest the system. We will gain better perspective on what is really dangerous, and what is an illusionary danger.

By the way, that mule ride ended up treating my fear of heights! Not that I recommend it as the best way to overcome your fear of heights.

SOME PRACTICAL ADVICE

When it comes to thrilling and scary hobbies, people highly vary in terms of what they consider as fun, what they think is too scary, and what they find boring. Given that there are so many factors at play in determining each person's experience of fear, it is important for everyone to know their own limits. We do not have to do things because of peer pressure, or because other people find them exciting even if we don't. It is not necessary to go to a haunted house or watch a horror movie if you find them too scary. Know yourself and go at your own pace, do not get bullied into it, and turn off the TV when you need to. Remember that the purpose is having fun. If it is not fun anymore, don't do it.

When you know and respect your limits, you might choose to push them a bit further and increase your tolerance of fear, for some added excitement.

Chapter 6

Courage Is Not the
Absence of Fear

You know what I learned in this war? It's absolutely normal not to have fear, yet to be afraid. . . . I have no fear towards the enemy, as paradoxically as it sounds. We should not allow fear to paralyze ourselves. But it's absolutely normal to be afraid of certain things.

—Dmytro Kulena, Ukraine minister of foreign affairs, on *The Late Show with Stephen Colbert*, September 22, 2022

We all want to be brave and admire bravery in others. Those who are perceived as brave are glorified in legends, history, culture, and the media. But there is no clear definition for courage and bravery, and what lies beneath the actions that are perceived as courageous could vastly vary depending on the case. The reasons people act against fear can even be contradicting. Some observers may see the same act as cowardice or even a crime, while others see it as heroism. This often happens in wars, when some see soldiers of a certain army as criminals, and the other side sees them as courageous heroes. As I am writing this chapter, the war in Ukraine is ongoing, and while most of the world sees the invading Russian forces as ruthless thugs, some in Russia receive their dead soldiers as heroes who died defending their delusional cause.

In attempting to narrow down the definition of courage, people have suggested terms like physical courage, bravery, or heroism. For example, while physical courage is acting against the risk of physical harm or death, heroism is defined as a prosocial action with risk to self.

But semantics aside, what is bravery and what constitutes being brave? What are the characteristics of brave people? How can we be braver? Do brave people not experience fear? Is it even good to not have any fear or anxiety in the face of danger?

The answer is capital letters NO! The inability to experience fear or anxiety is a terrible evolutionary disadvantage. The fact that healthy humans are capable of being scared suggests that those with genetic differences causing absence of fear lost their battle to natural selection. It is like the inability to sense pain. Those who are not able to sense pain are prone to severe injuries, infections, not feeling the disease in their body, all of which could be potentially catastrophic to their health. Lack of an ability to experience fear has been studied in animals. After scientists removed their amygdala on both sides of the brain, these animals lost their ability to learn fear, or show fear-related behavior such as escape or freezing. The rats would not react to the scent of a cat, and were not able to learn the association between a sound and a shock that could help them avoid the shock if they learned it. A fearless monkey would not be bothered by an approaching tiger or would feel too cozy and comfortable in proximity of an angry alpha monkey.

Humans with diseases or injuries leading to bilateral damage to the amygdala are unable to experience fear in potentially dangerous situations. They are even not able to perceive fear in other humans, or focus their attention on threat-related cues. In a very interesting experiment, scientists exposed a person with damage to both amygdalae to different situations that most other people would find difficult. She was very comfortable around scary exotic animals, didn't flinch at the haunted house, and did not find scary movies scary. She was drawn to the snakes and curiously wanted to hold them. Without any hesitation, she led the research team in the haunted house. None of the monsters could startle her; rather, her reaction was laughter and curiosity!

Although it sounds cool to not have any fear, the person in the above case study would have serious challenges in real-life situations of danger. Imagine trying to pet an angry barking dog, trying to have a fun conversation with a robber pointing a gun at you, or walking around in a war zone when missiles are coming down.

As we learned earlier, an important function of fear is preparing the whole body and the brain for focused, precise, and fast action by activation of the sympathetic system, heightened attention and arousal, brisk reactions. Lack of fear would take away all these evolutionary advantages when in danger. By now, I hope I have convinced you that lack of fear does not serve us well, and would not make good soldiers or heroes. Then, what is bravery?

> *Bran thought about it. "Can a man still be brave if he's afraid?" "That is the only time a man can be brave," his father told him.*
>
> —George R. R. Martin, *A Game of Thrones*

As absence of fear does not seem to be a good explanation for courage, fear is an integral part of being brave. In other words, courage and bravery only exist in the face of fear. A courageous person is tested against what seems to be scary and stops others from acting. So courage should either result from having less fear than others, or an ability to react to fear differently and control fear behavior. After all, an act of bravery is an observable behavior, and could have different—even at times contradicting—reasons. In other words, we often do not know what happens in the mind of a brave person; we just see their actions. However, for the brave act that we observe, there should either be reduced feeling of fear itself, or the resulting fear-related behavior such as avoidance, escape, or procrastination, to allow the person to act against what fear dictates. A soldier who jumps on a grenade to save the lives of his brothers should either be less scared than the others or able to better control the flight-or-freezing response.

As a trauma expert, I work a lot with first responders who have gone through extremely painful traumatic experiences. Once I was talking to a police officer who lost her partner, who was also one of her closest friends, in a shooting. She said that when she noticed her partner was shot in the neck and fell to the ground, she immediately ran to him and held her fingers on his bleeding jugular. Bullets were still coming down and she was not in cover. Then the shooter began walking toward her and her partner, but she was lucky enough that other cops arrived in time and saved her life. I asked her, "You went to save your partner without being able to take cover. Were you not worried about your life?" She answered, "I did not think about it!" She did not even see what she did as a courageous act; she could not see any other way to react. To her that was the normal thing to do, the right thing.

Although there are debates about the definitions of courage, for the sake of practicality we'll stick with the ability to act in the face of perceived danger, or what is perceived as dangerous by others. Also, we might be able to see that courage relates more with the *fight* aspect of fear, instead of the flight or freeze response, whether it is fighting a tangible threat, or taking action in the face of more abstract risks. From this angle, we might not definitely know what is happening in the mind and the body of the person executing an act of courage. Like in the case of this police officer, they themselves may not know the exact answer. Retrospective memory may not always be the most accurate; when we recall the memories, our brain and body are not in the state they were during the fight. Cultural and moral expectations may also require the courageous person to offer reasons that are more acceptable to the audience. Interestingly, and sadly, moral and cultural aspects of what is defined as courage may change over time. An example is Warrant Officer Hugh Thompson Jr., an American helicopter pilot who protected Vietnamese women and children during the war in Vietnam. At the time, he was perceived as a traitor. But as perceptions about the war changed, he was later awarded the Distinguished Flying Cross. Bottom line, we often cannot completely understand the underlying mechanisms of a brave action, or even if the person doing it was really feeling brave at the time.

MANY CAUSES OF COURAGE

To deconstruct bravery, we can go back to what we already know about fear and the factors that affect and modify it.

Threat Perception

The very first step in the experience of fear is perception of danger. Without imaginary or real danger, there is no fear. In this sense, one path to bravery is manipulation of the perceived level of danger. Even the exact same threat is perceived differently by different people. A lower level of perceived threat could help someone to act braver in comparison to the person who sees the situation as more dangerous. "Threat perception" has two aspects: (a) the threat itself, and (b) the perception. The *threat* is the objective level of danger, the statistical estimate of the level of risk of harm in a given dangerous situation, for example, trying to disarm a robber holding a knife. But even in the same situation, the statistical risk of harm can significantly differ based on the size, previous training, agility, distance, and many other physical and social circumstances of the two parties. A Navy SEAL would definitely face a much lower risk in this situation than I would.

Still the more complicated aspect is the *perception* of danger by the person deciding how to handle the situation. Let us now look at the factors that affect perception of threat.

An accurate threat appraisal is pivotal to survival and proper handling of the situation. Underestimation of danger could cost us dearly, and overestimation could lead to losing opportunities. While failing to run away from an angry predator could kill our ancestors, running away from a racoon would give their food away to the little thief. Both of these miscalculations could cost them their survival. Still, a person who illogically overestimates the risks could be seen as acting less brave, and someone who underestimates the danger could be seen as brave if they get lucky and survive the real danger. There is a Farsi proverb about the latter: "While the wise is calculating how to pass the deep river, the fool has already passed it!"

Our perception of the level of danger is not always accurate. While someone could perceive a disagreement with their superior as a potential catastrophe leading to loss of job, respect, and income, another person might just see it as a constructive discussion. These different perceptions would lead the first person to avoid any disagreement with the superior, and perceiving their colleague who does it as very brave in challenging authority.

Knowledge

For an accurate risk assessment, we need experience and knowledge, as well as the ability to process a multitude of contextual variables that affect the threat level. A zoologist who knows the signs that a wild animal has no intention of attacking or is even by nature scared of humans will feel comfortable and act more confident in the presence of that animal. In the eyes of the less experienced or informed person, the informed person may look very brave (have you seen the movie *Crocodile Dundee*?). For this expert, although there may be an instinctual fear response triggered, the contextual information processed in the prefrontal cortex and the hippocampus calms down the amygdala and then kills the fear.

The opposite happens when someone is not able to see how dangerous the situation really is. Someone who does not know that a wolverine can be vicious if you get near her cubs might look brave if they try to pet those fluffy little things, and get lucky because the mother is away.

(Perceived) Skills

Knowing how to handle a potentially dangerous situation and how to use the available tools and resources to deal with a scary situation is an important factor in fear. Medical training is arduous, and it requires gaining a lot of skills before one is comfortable dealing with a critical patient in the emergency room. During our training as medical doctors, my colleagues and I at times were terrified of being on our own in the emergency room, because we were worried we might not be skilled enough to handle the situation perfectly when a patient with a critical illness arrived. On the other hand, the attending physician was much more comfortable and fearless. She had enough experience to be able to handle most of the critical situations and, if in doubt, knew how to seek help in dealing with critically ill patients. When I was a junior resident in psychiatric training, a potentially violent, angry, psychotic patient was terrifying in the ER. But as I learned more about the signs of imminent aggression and gained better negotiation and empathic skills, I acted a lot more confident in these situations. I was the same person; what had changed was my skills. To us juniors, the attending physician seemed so brave. As we ourselves gained more experience during years of training, we learned more about different signs of escalating agitation and aggression in patients, and the resources available for our safety. Our brains triggered fewer false alarms, and we knew when and how to avoid harm when aggression was imminent.

Having done many similar drills, a trained Navy SEAL has already created the brain pathways of acting fast and effectively. They also know that they have a better chance of survival, as they have already practiced their action plans A to Z, and exit strategies from the dangerous situation.

Sense of Control

Real or perceived control has an important role in reducing fear and anxiety. Having an effective weapon in war, or an N95 mask when treating patients with a dangerous respiratory virus, gives a better sense of control over the feared threat. This is so important that often we even create an imaginary sense of control to overcome terror. We have always done this throughout the history of our species in the face of horrors of natural or human-caused disasters. A belief of being in control over our destiny and some ability to prevent the bad outcomes is so important that we have been willing to sacrifice our tribemates to gods and spirits so they would protect other members of the tribe. And we still do it. We pray, wear a wristband or a necklace, knock on wood, and do other scientifically unproven methods to feel like we can avoid what we are afraid of with these actions. Sometimes worrying itself gives us that sense of agency. I have noticed that for a lot of anxious patients, it feels like the act of worrying about something, in a magical way, reduces the chance of it happening. When they try to pause worrying for a minute, part of them, at a subconscious level, resists it because it believes worrying will prevent the disasters. That is why coming to terms with the reality that we actually have little control over most things in life could actually be liberating. Accepting what we cannot control stops us from fighting or creating illusions of control, and lets us focus on what we can change. This is one important element of being wisely brave.

Choosing the Lesser of Two Evils

There is a Farsi proverb that says, "I am taking refuge in a snake, from a dragon." Sometimes an act against fear is to avoid a larger perceived threat. A soldier may act against all the odds in the battlefield because he is afraid of worse punishment if he ignores the orders. On one hand, there is a fear of punishment of loss of income, prison, or even execution that will "definitely" happen if the order is ignored. On the other hand is a "likelihood" of injury or death if the order is followed. Revolutions are never accomplished by people who are happily enjoying life. That soldier might choose the potential harm to avoid guaranteed harm. People choose to risk imprisonment or death on the streets when they are really fed up with poverty, oppression, and injustice. Adversity, especially with perception of unfairness, often makes people braver, and more reckless about their safety. The worse is not always concrete and tangible like in the case of the soldier in this example, though. It could be a culturally deeply rooted fear of abandonment and shame, isolation, or going to hell if the war is considered religiously sanctioned. After all, it seems better to be shot and die than burn in hell for eternity, especially if you were raised with the image of most brutal tortures that sinners receive in hell. The fear of the greater evil has always been abused by leaders when convincing humans to commit horrible atrocities.

Purpose

Steve is a retired police officer, US Marshal, SWAT team member, full-time dad, husband, and coach. We successfully worked together to help him overcome PTSD. I have a picture of the two of us on my desk with writing on it: "Who is more handsome?" While we have still not found out the answer to this question, my admiration for his character is unquestionable. Like other first responders I have worked with, I have asked Steve about his reason for joining the force. These are not high-paying jobs and are extremely stressful with frequent exposure to the worst of what humans do to each other. His answer resonates with that of many other first responders. Growing up, he witnessed unfairness, bullying, and abuse in society. He wanted to protect people from these experiences, and was willing to risk being hurt for this cause. Steve has done CPR on a dying infant, has dealt with an active shooting, and has witnessed a car accident scene where the driver's brain was found on the back seat of the car. But for him, "the most traumatic are the ones where you cannot save people." Very often I hear from first responders that the thought of their own child is a great motivator in trying to save a young person.

We are creatures of meaning. Our interpretation of experiences—and the values we assign to them—largely impact our behavior and emotions. The meaning we attribute to each situation, via prefrontal pathways, can mitigate or increase the experience of fear in the amygdala. A Ukrainian soldier who is fighting for an honorable cause of protecting his people and homeland has a different perspective of the horrors of war and possibility of death than a Russian soldier who is fighting unjustly for Putin's delusional ambitions. During the invasion of Iran by Saddam's army (1980–1988), some Iranian soldiers volunteered to walk in the minefield to clear a path for their comrades. History is filled with examples of moral, cultural, spiritual, or patriotic causes for acts of heroism, and also atrocities. Sometimes the circumstances of what happened to the person are the reason they rise to the occasion against the predictions. An excellent example is how Ukrainian president Volodymyr Zelenskyy transformed from a former comedian to a war hero, so courageously against all bets and predictions of the international community. When the war started and he was offered exit from Ukraine by Western allies, he famously said, "I need ammunition, not a ride."

Biology

Our biological making of fear processing and emotion regulation can also play a role in the way we handle scary situations. Genetic differences in threat perception, emotion regulation, and baseline and reactive levels of anxiety are some of these variables. Some of us are biologically more reactive, and some are more laid back. Variable experiences of our ancestors with adversity could also be part of the epigenetic makeup of this difference. The epigenetic and biological brain differences could also be caused by our own previous experiences. Practice of emotion regulation skills also strengthen the brain's pathways over time. Some, the daredevils, are more inherently impulsive and less cognizant of danger. They are often less calculated in face of the danger, and their actions might seem more courageous. However, their reckless actions may be detrimental to themselves or others.

To summarize, what seems to be an act of courage could be the result of many different and often contradicting variables. Courage could be caused by wisdom and altruism, or impulsive miscalculation of danger or one's ability to handle it. Underestimation of risks or overestimation of one's ability to handle the situation is "bravery by ignorance." True courage, on the other hand, is the ability to act purposefully and accurately in face of danger and under stress. True courage requires a complicated process of threat estimation, precise risk assessment, calculation of possible outcomes, and consideration of one's abilities and resources, weighing in the risks and benefits of action or inaction to self and others.

Chapter 7

I'm Afraid, So I'm Angry

Fear and Aggression

Fear leads to anger. Anger leads to hate. Hate leads to suffering.

—Master Yoda

In September 2020, Brandon Gulish, a brilliant producer and now friend, came to my house to interview me for his independent film *The Elephants and the Grass*. This excellent documentary tells the story of a South Sudanese refugee young woman and her mother who went through the horrors of war and challenges of resettlement. Brandon wanted to talk to me because of my expertise in research and treatment of trauma in general, and more specifically in refugees. At some point during the interview, Brandon asked me an intriguing question: "Could personal experience of trauma play a role in the violence of the political leaders?" I had to pause and think; we usually do not look at aggression from this angle. Brutal dictators are often seen as fearless and tough, even referred to as "strong men." But fear (at least fear of loss of power and control) is a very important aspect of their thinking and decisions they make, and their perpetration of violence.

I would not do justice to a deep understanding of fear without addressing aggression and its closely knit relationship with fear. Indeed, fear is almost always a reaction to perception of anger, aggression, or violence aimed at the scared party. On the other hand, while anger, aggression, and violence might on the surface seem the opposite of fear, they themselves are often a reaction to fear. In my clinical practice when I notice anger in a patient, I first ask myself: "What are they afraid of? To what perceived threat are they reacting with anger? What are they trying to protect themselves from?" In this chapter I will explain the overlapping biology and psychology of aggression and fear, and their dynamics.

63

From an evolutionary standpoint, fear is there to protect us and ours from threats of harm. To avoid injury, death, or loss of resources, we have tools of fight and flight. Given the circumstances, sometimes we and other animals choose to attack the perceived danger, and sometimes we choose to run away. A scared animal or human dynamically and often automatically adjusts and switches between the two responses depending on what is more appropriate for self-preservation. And the "fight" does not necessarily have to be a full-blown attack. A cornered cat hisses, a frustrated dog shows its teeth and growls, and a kid yells at the bully to back off. They all hope that their signal is taken seriously enough that the other party will leave them alone. As the goal here is to scare off the opponent, they need a good understanding of how fear works in others. In other words, the aggressor needs an ability for empathy with the fear in their target. That is another close tie between fear and aggression, and that is how dictators use their own fear as a compass for how to terrify others.

What we have learned from research of fear and aggression is fascinating. For example, we know that in animals a choice between fear/escape and aggression depends on the developmental stage, sex, and internal hormonal states. Adult male rats are more likely to show aggressive behavior in response to certain odors than juvenile males, because for a less skilled and weaker rat pup, escape is more adaptive than engaging attacking a larger rat. Male sex hormones potentiate this aggression in adult male rats, which is absent in castrated males. Lactating female rats are also more aggressive. This is because the pups are not as mobile as the mother, and if mother escaped, the pups would face the risk of being eaten by predators or killed by other rats.

In us humans, anger presents itself in more diverse and complicated ways. It can range from an awareness of the emotion in our head and body without expressing it, to showing an angry face or other nonverbal cues, to verbal expression of anger or intention of aggression, to physical acts of violence. Aggression can be abstract and symbolic, like blocking someone on social media, or when it is expressed in the form of art and literature. Sometimes people are not even aware of their anger, like the person who shouts, "I am not angry!" Anger that is triggered by fear not only can fool others, but also the scared person themselves.

When in danger, we must act fast; that is why fear is more impulsive than logical. Also, in the face of threats, false alarms are okay. If there is a 10 percent chance there is a predator behind the bushes, running away is still wise, although 90 percent of the time it will be a waste of energy. The same applies to aggression in response to a perceived threat. When our ancestors faced a potentially (but not definitely) dangerous animal, if they could, they would try to kill it. Because some snakes were venomous, they would kill all the snakes that entered their cave. Like fear, anger also has to be fast and impulsive, and less logical.

OVERLAPPING NEUROBIOLOGY

When we are angry and when we are scared, we experience overlapping mental and physical reactions. That is because for both fight and flight, we need to focus our energy and resources on physical actions needed for fleeing or attacking the perceived source of danger. Mentally, we become alert, and our attention is overly focused on what scares or angers us and away from other things. A soldier patrolling the war zone does not pay attention to flowers and the beautiful sky, but the movements in the bushes would grasp his attention. The mind will not stop thinking about the perceived threat and potential ways of neutralizing it, until it is gone. That is why we keep brewing about what scares or angers us; both emotions are deeply engaging and are hard to shake off. Physical symptoms of an activated sympathetic nervous system are shared between fear and aggression: muscles are tense, breathing is heavy, heart rate is increased, and we are more easily startled. This is because the evolutionary outcomes of both fear and anger would be very similar: physical action away from or toward the perceived threat. Like fear, anger and aggression heavily engage the amygdala both in animals and humans. The prefrontal cortex takes part in regulation and control of anger, and its diminished activity and size is found to correlate with more aggressive behavior. Interestingly, researchers have also observed large amygdala responses to perception of both fear and anger in others. In fMRI studies, when the participants were shown images of angry or fearful human faces, their amygdala showed a larger reaction than when they saw neutral faces. For social beings like us, both fear and anger in other humans signal that something bad might be about to happen to us or ours. An angry human looking at us might be about to attack us, and the scared face of our tribemate might signal that something dangerous is about to happen to both of us. In both cases, the amygdala warns the rest of the brain and the body, to prepare us for action. Perception of fear- or anger-related behaviors in others also leads to activation of the amygdala. So not only do our own and others' emotions of fear and anger trigger a common response, but also perception of these emotions in others triggers that reaction in our brain. Interestingly, in anxious people, or those with previous experience of trauma and adversity, we observe an increased amygdala response to both angry and fearful faces. This means these brains are conditioned to be more alert and wary of any potential sign of danger, due to previous exposure to such threats. Our research team has found that those adults who were raised in an environment of poverty had a larger amygdala response to both angry and fearful faces and smaller response to happy faces, compared to those who were raised in a middle-income family. We speculated that exposure to a harsher environment that often accompanies poverty during childhood sensitizes the brain to signs of danger, at the cost of not noticing the more positive cues as much.

At the chemical level in the brain, dopamine and norepinephrine are both involved in heightened states of arousal of fear and anger. In animal studies, brain dopamine level is increased both in anticipation of aggression, and after violent behavior. Serotonin is implicated in aggressive and violent behavior, and fear and anxiety. Low levels of serotonin have been found in brains of both animals and humans with aggressive behavior toward self or others. More violent methods of suicide are linked with a lower level of serotonin in the brain. Interestingly, medications such as selective serotonin reuptake inhibitors (SSRIs) that modulate serotonin function in the brain (more in chapter 10) are used in treatment for both anxiety and impulsive behaviors, and can potentially reduce aggression.

Hormonal levels can also affect the way our brains process danger cues. In an interesting study, Austrian researchers found that males' testosterone level was correlated with the level of amygdala response to view of both fearful and angry faces: the higher the testosterone level, the larger the amygdala response to faces signaling danger. Similarly, testosterone is linked with increased aggressive behavior. During both anxiety and aggression, stress hormone cortisol level increases both in animals and humans. A reduced level of oxytocin (famously known as the love hormone) has been observed in aggressive animals.

FEAR AND HISTORY OF EXPOSURE TO VIOLENCE

Research has shown that exposure to aggression and violence has a long-term impact on fear brain and experience of fear, even long after the source of aggression is gone. We are primed to make long-standing memories of highly dangerous experiences, to ensure that we will avoid them in future encounters. A painful experience with a wolf should forever prevent us from trying to pet any animal looking like the predator again. Fear generalization is often a mechanism via which exposure to aggression and violence leads to long-standing fear and anxiety, and a general state of threat awareness and heightened arousal. As I will extensively discuss in chapter 9, posttraumatic stress disorder or PTSD is an extreme result of traumatic and violent experiences. But violence can also lead to more subtle changes in the brain and behavior, like hypervigilance to any sign of danger, and increased anxiety. Those learned, overly cautious behaviors and avoidance might not always be appropriate or relevant anymore and may cost us opportunities. In my clinic, I often help my patients get rid of these old fears of past experiences that block them from freely maximizing their potential for a prosperous life. For example, many people who have experienced abusive relationships in the past—even decades earlier—tend to avoid seeking a relationship out of fear of being trapped in the same experience. Paradoxically, being too scared and cautious can also open the door to future abuse and bullying. School bullies always target kids who are more timid and easily scared. And that can cause a negative cycle of being bullied and abused once one has had a painful experience with peers.

Over the past decade, childhood exposure to trauma and adversity has become a focus of mounting research, and every day we are learning more about the potential lifelong impact of such exposure on mental and physical health and behavior. My colleague and friend Dr. Tanja Jovanovic and her team showed, in a study published in 2020, that exposure to violence in children can change the anatomy and function of the amygdala, hippocampus, and prefrontal cortex, which are major players in fear processing. The effects on brain processing and resulting emotions and behavior could be so subtle and often subconscious that the person may not even be aware of them. They might just find themselves uncomfortable in some contexts, or want to run away or avoid without knowing why. In another interesting study, one group of participants was shown pictures of community violence, and the other group saw neutral images. After that, both groups went through a Pavlovian fear conditioning and extinction learning paradigm. The researchers found that the participants who saw violent pictures before fear conditioning had a higher skin conductance response (a measure of sympathetic reactivity indicative of automatic fear) to the conditioned stimulus. This means that exposure to violence can strengthen learning of fear and danger in future experiences. Once scared, we will be more scared the next time. Importantly, in this study extinction learning was also weaker, suggesting an impaired ability to learn that a previously dangerous stimulus is not dangerous anymore. Or once scared, next time feeling safe will be harder.

AGGRESSION IN RESPONSE TO FEAR

Aggression could also result from fear and be an attempt in protecting self against perceived danger. As the purpose of fear is to detect the threat and then calculate the actions that help us survive it, one possible outcome of this calculation is aggression and violence. There is no one formula to how decisions are made by each person regarding aggression versus flight and avoidance. Here are some of the major variables that determine if a response should be tilted toward fear (flight) or aggression (fight):

Sense of Control

Many years ago, I was in the backyard with my late black Labrador Hailey when she noticed an opossum. Hailey did not have boundaries when it came to two things: food and curiosity. She naturally approached the opossum, and it chose to play dead. But Hailey kept on getting closer and started sniffing the animal. As the little guy saw no respect for its boundaries by this curious dog, it switched to showing teeth while still lying on the ground. When that did not work, it barged at Hailey, and ran away when she backed off.

As lack of a sense of control is an important determinant of fear and anxiety, and because fear and aggression go hand in hand, lack of control, or not seeing a way out, increases the potential for aggression. That is true for animals, but also for humans. A skilled and experienced security officer who feels confident in their ability to tackle a violent person holding a knife may be less likely to pull the trigger than an untrained citizen with a firearm in the same situation. In this scenario, a calculated perception of one's ability to handle the situation not only reduces the risk of aggression, but also its scale. Said officer may use force to stop the perpetrator, but less violently and in a more controlled manner. A lower sense of control even impacts our appraisal of threats and their level of intensity. Things appear to be scarier when we feel a lack of agency. Researchers have found that people with a lower sense of control are more likely to perceive a neutral facial expression as angry, and to report more aggressive behavior via increased perception of threat. Sadly, there is also a cycle of exposure to aggression and abuse, and reduced sense of control. For example, children with chronic exposure to childhood abuse have been found to perceive external control as stronger than their own internal control and a sense of agency. That means they feel that external forces have a larger impact on their life than their own determination.

There is, however, another side to the connection between control and aggression. Too much power in the wrong hands can increase use of force, violence, and aggression. In people with a tendency for violence or criminal activity, fear of retribution is an important factor in preventing or limiting their aggression. A historically famous research study on control and aggression is the Milgram experiment. In this experiment, the participants were made to believe that they could administer a desired level of shock to another person, an actor who was not really receiving any shock, but acted as if in agony in proportion to the level of shock administered. The researchers found that many of their participants, regular citizens recruited for this study, were willing and able to administer the maximum amount of shock to another human being when they were given full control over the level of shock and permission to use it. Of note, this study would probably not be approved by a research review board in our time because of serious ethical concerns surrounding it.

Human history is filled with real-world examples of this experiment. Absent fear of retribution, countless dictators and tyrants have not hesitated to inflict suffering, torture, and death on millions of innocent people for their delusional ambitions.

Love, Caring, and Hormones

When I was a child, I was visiting a village in Iran with my family on a holiday weekend. At that time in Iran, people rarely had pet dogs in houses, and dogs were mostly used for guarding farms, sheep, and orchards. I saw a domesticated dog sitting calmly in a corner with her pups. She looked so friendly that I allowed myself to approach and try to pet the puppies. That was a terrible decision. I still have a vivid memory of how she immediately shifted to loudly barking, warning me to back off.

Maternal aggression is a very interesting phenomenon in animals, the purpose of which is protecting the offspring. Maternal aggressive behavior has been extensively researched in rats, a weaker species that normally uses freezing and escape in response to danger. But interestingly, when it comes to a risk to the pups, mom cannot run away; she must stay and fight. The hormonal changes that happen during and after pregnancy play a main role in this change in behavior, which lingers until around the time the pups are more mobile. As the pups grow older and more capable of fleeing, mom can also gradually return to her baseline behavior. Very interestingly, mother's own scary experiences during infancy affect her maternal aggression. For example, a group of researchers found that female rats that were intermittently separated from their own mother during infancy (which you can imagine is a stressful experience for a pup) tended to be more afraid, and as a result more aggressive in protecting their own pups!

Uncertainty

Uncertainty is another important contributor to fear, which also impacts violence and aggression. Uncertainty about the extent and likelihood of threat, and an inability to predict behavior of the opponent, increase *preemptive aggression*. Preemptive aggression is an attempt to remove or reduce the threat before the adversary gets a chance to act. Uncertainty increases fear, and fear needs fast and impulsive response, and often resorts to violence. Preemptive aggression is a very complicated aspect of international politics, especially when it comes to the worst possible outcomes, including nuclear confrontations. If the leader of one of the nuclear superpowers determines that the other is about to launch a nuclear strike, they will only have a few minutes to act and launch a full-scale nuclear attack to ensure destruction of the adversary. The "mutual assured destruction doctrine" speculates that a nuclear attack on another nuclear power will lead to complete annihilation of both parties, which is believed to prevent the attacker from taking the risk. But in such high-stakes situations, any misunderstanding can lead to a catastrophe threatening our species. To curtail the risk of miscalculations based on uncertainties, superpowers always try to keep a line of communication open even with their worst adversaries. As I am writing this chapter, the US and Russia are still in touch, despite the Russian invasion, and full support of the US for Ukraine.

Intensity of Perceived Threats

As a nuclear attack is the most destructive military action, a response to it also must be most aggressive: full-scale nuclear assault to annihilate the perpetrator. The level of threat, and what can be lost, is another determinant of fear-based aggression. Facing a robber holding a gun, most of us would not risk it, and would just give them our wallet. But if we suspect that the intruder might want to kill us or our loved ones, we are more likely to try to attack first. Understandably, most of such high-stakes situations are also uncertain (real-life villains are usually less clear about their violent intentions than those in the movies), and split-second decisions are often made based on guesses.

Past Experiences

Past experiences play an important role in how people handle fear, including their potential use of aggression. Research shows that those with previous exposure to violence to themselves are more likely to use violent methods for resolving conflict. We not only learn fear from others via observation, but also learn when and how to use aggression in reaction to a perceived threat. Repeated early life exposure to violence as the main method for conflict resolution by caregivers, especially in the absence of more mature and adaptive ways of coping with stressful situations, teaches the child that is the only way to win and avoid loss. Lack of learned skills for proper risk assessment, negotiating disagreements and challenges, and emotion regulation increases the likelihood of use of violence in response to conflict. Through exposure to bullying, partner abuse, parental violence, and a culture of war, youth learn that violence and aggression is the way to achieving their goals and protecting themselves. On a larger scale, intergenerational transmission of violence creates a negative cycle of aggression among groups, nations, and their leaders. Those whose childhood and political career have been filled with observing brutality, violence, and coups might see it as the only way of resolving conflict and overcoming fear of annihilation or loss of power and control.

It is important to emphasize that what I am doing here is trying to explain, and not justify, the fear roots of violence and aggression. This chapter was a long answer to Brandon Gulish's thoughtful question during that interview for his documentary.

Chapter 8

Diseases of Fear and Anxiety

When I leave work, I am so worried that I might have unknowingly bumped into someone and injured them, that I have to drive back to my workplace and check everyone to make sure nobody is hurt.

—Patient with OCD

Over the centuries, our perception of abnormal, disease, and disorder has largely evolved. Religion, philosophy, anthropology, and experimental sciences have long contemplated about the definition of normal. When it comes to human emotions, thoughts, and behaviors, the distinction is even harder, because often the disease is an exaggeration of what is normal. For example, in infectious disease medicine, one either is or is not infected with a specific germ or virus. But psychiatric illnesses are more like hypertension (high blood pressure): every human alive has a level of blood pressure detectable in their arteries, caused by the nonstop pumping of the heart. A person with no blood pressure is a dead person. If the blood pressure passes a certain level beyond what is seen in an average healthy person, then it is considered abnormal. There is a spectrum of blood pressure from borderline to mild to moderate to severe hypertension. Same is true about most psychiatric illnesses, especially fear-, anxiety-, and trauma-related disorders. All healthy humans at times and in reaction to life circumstance experience fear, stress, and anxiety, and many are exposed to trauma. However, not all who feel scared or anxious have a mental illness or a disordered fear system. That brings us to a fundamental question: What is abnormal?

WHAT IS ABNORMAL?

I often remind my medical students and psychiatry trainees of the importance of differentiating between abnormal fear and anxiety, and normal human

73

reactions to what should be stressful or scary. There are times when we must be scared or stressed. For example, if someone is in a physically abusive relationship, being afraid and anxious is a normal reaction to an ongoing risk of harm and experience of pain and humiliation. The right intervention in this case is not prescribing antianxiety medications. The right thing is to help the person safely leave that abusive relationship. In this case fear is doing what it is supposed to do: to warn to be alert against the active threat. For an employee who is stressed and anxious in a punitive, harassing, and unfriendly work environment, that anxiety is a signal that they must try to change those work circumstances, or leave that job. In these examples, it would be unwise for a clinician to use medications in an attempt to numb the person's negative emotions. In other words, sometimes anxiety is the pin in the wrong chair that we are sitting on, that is telling us we must get off the chair.

As our scientific methods, thinking, and cultural values have changed over time, so has our definition of normal and abnormal. We have gradually moved away from hypothetical, ideological, philosophical, and religious definitions for normal and abnormal, to a more evidence-based and "functional" approach that focuses on a person's capacity for happiness and functioning. I teach my trainees that in contemporary psychiatry, the main guide for intervention is (a) patient's impaired functioning in major life areas, and (b) their experience of distress and agony.

But how do we decide what is dysfunctional, and how much stress is too much? One common way is looking at the "average" human response to a similar situation, and how most people would handle it. For example, while many people do not like spiders, only a minority are terrified of spiders to the point they would sleep on the couch if they found a spider in their bedroom.

Real versus Perceived Danger

One difference between a normal reaction to potentially harmful situations and abnormal fear is what causes it. Most patients with phobias know themselves that their fears are irrational. They even sometimes say, "I know it is stupid, but I am afraid of X, Y, and Z." It makes sense to be terrified at the sight of a wolf in the woods, but most people are not afraid of a domesticated dog. The distinction between what is really dangerous and what we wrongly perceive as dangerous is a key in this determination.

For abstract thinking beings like humans, whether a perceived threat is real or not is often complicated. Many threats of modern life are not as concrete as facing a predator or a snake. We deal with a variety of complex situations and concepts in the environmental, social, political, and cultural spheres. For example, how much should we be afraid of acquiring a potentially life-threatening infection like the coronavirus? How much precaution in social life to avoid the infection is too much? How much handwashing, sanitizing, or testing is too much? In the current state of international affairs, how much should we be afraid of a nuclear war in the height of the tensions between nuclear superpowers? How important is our social standing and others' perception of us, and how much should we worry about it? Is it normal or abnormal to lose sleep the night before a decisive meeting with our boss? Even the answer to the same questions can change over time depending on how much we know about a certain threat. For example, the guidelines for preventing the COVID-19 infection largely varied in different countries when the pandemic began, and then changed over time as we learned more about the virus, and people got vaccinated.

An important aspect of treating fear and anxiety is to help the patients answer these questions and determine how realistic their fears are, and how adaptive the measures they are taking to protect themselves against the perceived danger are.

Dysfunction or Distress

Dysfunction and/or distress are always required before we can make a diagnosis of any mental illness. That means, if someone has symptoms of what is considered an illness but does not experience high levels of dysfunction or distress because of these symptoms, we do not deem them in need for clinical attention. Most often such a person does not even seek treatment unless they are curious to rule out possibility of an illness. So even if a behavior is a deviation from the "average," it is not considered an illness without the above conditions. Dysfunction could affect multiple areas of one's life from academic and occupational to social and personal functioning. For example, for most people, experiencing some degree of anxiety before an important exam is normal. Some anxiety is even helpful in creating the optimal level of arousal and attentiveness needed for performing better in an exam. But when the anxiety is so high that it impairs one's ability to focus or use their memory appropriately, it becomes unproductive and dysfunctional. If a person's social shyness does not negatively impact their ability to interact with others, then this shyness is not considered pathological, unless they are able to function only under a high level of subjective distress.

Subjective distress is the other important diagnostic aspect of mental illness, even in the absence of a significant level of dysfunction. While it is often easier to objectively assess a person's ability to function, experience of distress is something more subjective and often is not easily observable by others. Specifically, anxious people are often very skilled in concealing their anxiety, to the point that even a skilled psychiatrist might not notice it in a nonclinical context. I am an expert in anxiety and trauma, but I have often been surprised when a very calm-looking acquaintance opens up to me about their anxiety. Reliance on the subjective level of fear, anxiety, and distress is a major distinction between psychiatry and other fields of medicine. For example, while we can measure a patient's blood pressure or sugar level, we cannot put a cuff on their arm, or scan their brain to measure how anxious they are. Psychiatric diagnoses are mostly made based on clinical interviews, hearing the subjective report of the patients, and observing their behavior and patterns of functioning in life. In contrast, a patient with high blood pressure or diabetes might not even be aware of their illness.

To summarize, fear and anxiety are considered disordered only when they are disproportional to real-life circumstances, and cause significant level of distress and/or dysfunction.

The rest of this chapter will cover major disorders of fear and anxiety. I will explain these disorders, their symptoms, and the accompanying biological changes in the brain and the body. While most of these disorders are categorized under "anxiety disorders," some like phobias are more fear related with clearly defined feared situations causing them, and some consist more of anxiety and worries. But first let us look at the tools that we use in the clinic to make a psychiatric diagnosis.

CRITERION-BASED DIAGNOSIS

We use a criterion-based system for diagnosing mental illnesses, including anxiety disorders. For each mental disorder, there is a constellation of symptoms that need to be present before we can make that diagnosis. For example, for diagnosing generalized anxiety disorder (more below), the American Psychiatric Association (APA) requires presence of excessive worrying that is difficult to control, and at least three of the six symptoms of restlessness, being easily fatigued, poor concentration, irritability, muscle tension, and difficulty sleeping. These symptoms must be present for at least six months, cause significant distress or dysfunction, and not be caused by a medical illness or substance use. Most clinicians across the globe use one of two diagnostic systems: *DSM* (*Diagnostic and Statistical Manual of Mental Disorders*) by the APA, and International Classification of Diseases (ICD) by the World Health Organization. None of these methods is superior to the other, but as an American-trained psychiatrist, in this book I will use the APA's *DSM* guideline.

The criterion-based diagnostic systems allow clinicians and researchers to share a common language. For example, when I publish research data on prevalence of PTSD among refugees whom I work with, another scientist researching refugee mental health in Turkey will know what guideline I used for making the diagnosis, and our research findings become more easily comparable. While this is helpful for scientific and billing purposes (insurances require us to use these universal diagnostic systems in documentation), it is important to know anxiety does not work within confines of *DSM* or ICD. For example, someone might not have all the required symptoms for generalized anxiety disorder, but still be distressed by excessive worrying, poor concentration, and muscle tension (two, instead of three out of the six symptoms). On the spectrum of anxiety symptoms' severity, *DSM* draws an imaginary threshold line at some level of intensity to define a diagnosis. This does not mean that people who have a slightly lower number of the symptoms cannot be distressed or dysfunctional. In real-life clinical practice, our focus is on distress and dysfunction in determining who needs what kind of help.

It is also important to note that this and the next two chapters are not written with the intent of training the reader to diagnose these illnesses in themselves and others, or try to treat them. Like other medical conditions, that must be left to trained clinicians. My hope from writing these chapters is for the readers to not only inform themselves, but also consider seeking evaluation and help if they are distressed by these symptoms. More importantly, I want them to know that help is available, and as I will explain in chapter 10, we can help a lot.

PREVALENCE

As fear is a hardwired core function of every human's psyche, it should not be surprising to know that fear-and-anxiety-related disorders are very common. According to large national studies, one in five (19 percent) American adults have experienced an anxiety disorder over the past year, and about one-third of them have met a diagnosis of an anxiety disorder at some point in their life. Now let us look at each of these disorders more closely. Of note, the prevalence of anxiety disorders is relatively similar across different countries, suggesting the universality of these issues.

SPECIFIC PHOBIAS

The hallmark of specific phobias is excessive, disproportionate, and unrealistic fear of an object or situation. Most patients do their best to avoid the feared situations at any cost. For example, I have seen patients with fear of flying who became very anxious and had a panic attack when on a plane, or lost sleep the nights and weeks before an anticipated flight. Some of them would have to travel for days from the east to the west coast of the country because their fear of being on a plane was unbearable.

Not liking spiders and sitting a few feet away from them does not necessarily constitute a diagnosis of arachnophobia, or fear of spiders. But I have diagnosed people with this condition who would not sleep in their bed or take a shower if they saw a spider in the bedroom or the shower, were not willing to step in the basement or go to a park for fear of possibility of an encounter with a spider. Phobias are very diverse and include countless objects and situations. Some of the most common phobias are fear of animals and insects (spiders, snakes, bugs, dogs); flying; heights; clowns; driving; vomiting; blood, injection, or injury; or enclosed spaces (claustrophobia).

Specific phobias are among the most common mental disorders and affect more than 10 percent of the US adult population. The level of dysfunction in phobias usually depends on the likelihood of an encounter. For example, someone with fear of snakes who lives in the cold state of Michigan will not have as much trouble as someone living in Texas. Someone with fear of flying who does not need to travel, or travels once every ten years, will be less distressed than a marketer who must travel several times a week.

Expectedly, sympathetic hyperactivity is an integral part of the phobic reaction. The fight-or-flight system activates to prepare the person for the flight. But interestingly, there is one phobia that works in a different direction: blood, injury, and injection phobia! When people with this phobia see blood or injury in themselves or others, or anticipate or receive an injection, the parasympathetic system activates, leading to a freezing response. Their blood pressure and heart rate lower, and they often faint! This could be an exaggerated adaptive evolutionary response. After serious injury, stopping the struggle may help reduce bleeding and further injury to vital organs.

Phobias often start at an early age, and there are different ways they can develop. Most of the time, though, we cannot pinpoint a clear cause for them. When we can determine a cause, like other learned fears, phobias can develop via personal experience (associative learning), for example, a terrifying experience with an aggressive dog in childhood. The problem with phobias is overgeneralization of the fear learning, leading to a fear of all dogs. The extent of the overgeneralization will determine the situations the phobic person will avoid. Depending on the often random associations made in their brain, a survivor of a serious car accident might avoid driving on the expressway, being the driver, being the passenger, being in a car in the rain, or being in a car altogether. It is hard to know what determines who will overgeneralize and develop a phobia after an adverse experience, but the intensity and unexpectedness of the danger and person's biological tendency for fear and anxiety can play a part.

People can also learn phobias from others' scary experiences, like seeing someone being bitten by a dog or injured in a car accident. Learning from others can also happen via exposure to their phobic behavior. I have previously referred to the story of the patient who was afraid of dogs because as a child, his mother acted very nervous any time she noticed a dog in the distance. She had also told him repeatedly that dogs are unpredictable even when they look friendly, and that a dog seriously injured a neighbor's child. Due to their own limited experience, children rely largely on their parents' advice regarding potential danger. My patient's reliance on his mom's risk assessment had prevented him from learning from his own experience how to interact with pet dogs. This avoidant behavior in phobic people often takes away the opportunities of learning skills (here of interacting with dogs) and gaining a sense of control and agency by experience.

The major brain areas that are involved in phobias are understandably the amygdala (fear response) and the insula (awareness of being afraid). Because of the primary involvement of the primitive brain, the fear response in phobias is usually automatic and subconscious. Often the phobic patient is even logically aware that their fear is not proportional to reality. In other words, the animal brain does it. I have repeatedly heard from my patients, "I know it is stupid, but I am afraid of X, Y, or Z." To which I have answered, "It is not stupid, it is illogical. Our brain has different functions, one of which is logical reasoning." As I will explain in chapter 10, phobias are usually easily treatable. Unfortunately, most people with phobias are not aware that their condition can be treated—often cured—and do not seek appropriate treatment.

SOCIAL PHOBIA

Social phobia, or social anxiety disorder, is a common and disabling anxiety disorder. As its name suggests, it is a condition of excessive anxiety in social situations. People with social phobia find it very difficult to be around others, especially strangers. That is mostly because they are very much worried about being judged or criticized by others, doing something embarrassing, or disappointing others. They are overly attentive to any sign in their social environment that people do not like them, or negatively judge them. If at a party someone does not smile at them or notice what they said because of the loud music, they might think she finds them boring or not interesting. If she does smile, they might think she is smirking because they did something stupid and embarrassingly funny. This negative interpretation of social interactions makes them more anxious, defensive, or withdrawing, which in turn makes the situation even more awkward. The other person will feel the weirdness of the situation and so becomes uncomfortable and withdraws. This will then confirm our social phobic person's theory that others don't like and avoid them. This often results in more withdrawal from social situations, and not gaining necessary skills for normal social functioning. People with social phobia might be afraid of being judged, doing something embarrassing or stupid, being boring, or showing embarrassing physical signs of anxiety such as getting blushed, pale, sweaty, or shaky, or having stomach upset in front of others. Of note, they do not feel anxious around their friends and family and in familiar social contexts.

Social phobia is very common, affecting 12 percent of the US population and is more common among women and girls. It often starts in childhood, teenage years, or early adulthood, a critical developmental stage when many of important life decisions and directions are consolidated. That is why this illness can tremendously impact one's life trajectory and their future, especially as our lives are very much intertwined with others. Imagine a very bright and nice teenager who is terrified of being judged by others. They will try their best to stay low key in school, and will not volunteer to answer questions, and are terrified of going to the front of the class. Because of being too shy and timid, they could be targeted by the bullies who will further damage their self-esteem and trust in others. They will avoid dating, and later will have difficulty choosing education and careers that require close frequent interactions with others. This all can lead to enormous loss of life opportunities if this condition is not treated. I have had patients who have avoided great life opportunities, or even dropped out of college, only because they were terrified of being in a class with others and joining group discussions.

It is important to differentiate social phobia from other conditions with avoidance of social interactions. For example, normal childhood or teenage shyness, if not causing significant distress or dysfunction, is not an illness. There are also other mental illnesses that may resemble social anxiety. For example, people with autism spectrum disorders often are not interested in social interactions or find them awkward because they are not able to connect well with others or read the social cues and follow social interactions. I have had patients who were referred to me with a diagnosis of social phobia, but turned out to be on the autism spectrum and were just not interested in others. What helps differentiate the two conditions is the cause of the avoidance: social phobic people often would love to be around others, but would avoid them out of fear of being judged. They are also much better in reading social cues—actually, reading "too much" into them. Sometimes psychotic disorders like schizophrenia cause avoiding others due to paranoid thoughts that others may want to harm the patient.

Like other anxiety disorders, social phobia shows increased amygdala and insula activation. In research studies, people with social phobia show greater attention to angry or fearful faces, compared to happy faces. They also tend to interpret neutral faces as having a negative affect. In summary, the socially phobic brain is constantly looking for signs of social disapproval in the environment.

We still do not know for sure what causes social phobia, but we have theories. People with a biological tendency for anxiety are more likely to develop social phobia. Genetic differences in processing of serotonin, norepinephrine, and dopamine in the brain could be a contributor, and lead to familial inheritance of the disorder. However, the familial aspect is also learned. Like other things, children learn about the social world, how safe or scary it is, and how to interact with it from their parents. If parents are often anxious around social contexts or avoid these situations, that signals to their children that there is something scary about people. They can also learn the beliefs of their parents, for example, that other people are always judgmental, their opinion is too important, and making mistakes in front of others is terribly embarrassing.

When parents are anxious and avoid social contexts, their children also will not have a chance to learn adaptive social skills from their parents by modeling, or by their own experience and practice. Overprotective parents also limit their children's chances of gaining social autonomy and learning social skills by engagement with peers during childhood. Harsh childhood experiences like judgmental and critical parenting, bullying, or medical conditions limiting their ability to engage with other children are other contributors.

It is very important to note that none of this means that all people with social phobia have bad parents. I often have to assure overly worried parents that their child's anxiety or other mental illness, even as an adult, is not their fault. Despite what the old-school psychoanalytic pop culture might have suggested, while parenting is very important in who we become, not all of our problems are the fault of our mothers! There are many different factors, some even unknown to science, that can lead to development of any anxiety disorder, including social phobia. It is important for parents of children with social phobia to not feel they are the only reason for their child's illness.

The recent COVID-19 pandemic has had a catastrophic impact on the social abilities of many children globally. The pandemic led to more than a year of remote schooling, total disconnect between families and the outside world, and lack of a chance for children to connect with their peers in this extremely stressful time. Many people's social behaviors and habits changed permanently even after the pandemic slowed down, and many still have very restricted social lives. During this highly important developmental time, many children have missed—and continue to miss—the chance of learning skills of social life. We will in the coming years learn more about the depth and vastness of the impact of the pandemic on children's social abilities and potentially higher levels of social anxiety.

Like other anxiety disorders, we have effective treatments for social phobia in the form of psychotherapy and safe medications, which I will explain in chapter 10. It is important to get treatment as soon as possible to mitigate long-term negative impact of the illness on a young person's ability to gain social skills and live their life to their full potential.

PANIC DISORDER

Panic disorder's hallmark is repeated "panic attacks." A panic attack is an acute occurrence of severe full-blown fear and anxiety, most often coming out of the blue. The attacks flare up rapidly and disappear in a few minutes. Patients experience intense fear and anxiety along with a variety of physical symptoms including pounding heart, shortness of breath, hyperventilation, chest tightness, nausea and sometimes vomiting, shaking, sweating, dizziness, and numbness and tingling in the extremities. The first few times the person is often terrified they might be having a stroke or a heart attack, or are about to die.

Having a panic attack does not necessarily mean having panic disorder. There are a lot of other conditions that can cause a panic attack. For example, a person with a phobia who encounters what they are afraid of, or someone with PTSD who is triggered by trauma memories, can experience a panic attack. What defines panic disorder is that the attacks are frequent and are not triggered externally. As panic attacks are not predictable, people with panic disorder are often worried about having an attack, especially in situations that can lead to embarrassment or are not easy to leave. As a result, they begin to avoid social situations such as gatherings, movie theaters, or restaurants, and some eventually end up isolated at home. Avoiding places and social contexts out of fear of having a panic attack is called agoraphobia (in Latin it means fear of the marketplace). Agoraphobia is often a result of panic disorder.

Understandably, most people with panic disorder are first seen in the emergency room, or by their primary care doctor or internist, because they think they are having a heart attack or a serious medical condition. That is actually good, because before diagnosing panic disorder, we need a medical evaluation to rule out medical conditions that can cause similar symptoms. Heart attack, stroke, diabetes, severe high blood pressure, and diseases of the adrenal or thyroid gland are some medical conditions that can resemble panic attacks. When medical causes are ruled out, the patient is often referred to mental health providers for appropriate treatment.

The brain signature of panic disorder is like phobias, with increased activation in the amygdala and insula, and a hyperactive sympathetic nervous system.

GENERALIZED ANXIETY DISORDER

While phobias and social phobia have clear, identifiable external triggers, generalized anxiety disorder, or GAD, is characterized by excessive worrying about a wide range of things. People with GAD basically worry about everything, all the time. They worry about health, safety, work, school, family, relationships, finances, past, future, everything. Most of the time their mind is occupied with all the things that could go wrong, and the worst possible outcomes for themselves and for their loved ones. When there is a real reason to worry, they will worry more than they need to. And when that issue is resolved, the anxious brain will find other things to worry about. The GAD brain will never stop ruminating about what could go wrong.

GAD affects about 6 percent of the general population and is more common among women. Other common symptoms besides excessive worrying include restlessness, poor concentration, feeling tired and fatigued, muscle tension, chest tightness, shortness of breath, sweating, and difficulty sleeping. Poor concentration is because part of the mind is always busy worrying about something in the background, which does not allow presence in the moment and focus on the task at hand. The anxious brain/mind is always in the future or the past, missing out on the now. The constant worrying eats up the mental energy, exhausts the system, and causes fatigue and tiredness. Nighttime worries do not allow the person to fall asleep.

An interesting observation I have had with GAD patients is that somewhere in the back of their mind, they believe that the act of worrying itself prevents the bad outcomes from happening. As if they stop worrying, their fears are more likely to happen, or they will not be prepared when they happen. This magical thinking limits their ability to stop worrying even for a short time.

People sometimes confuse GAD with attention deficit hyperactivity disorder (ADHD or ADD), because both disorders cause poor attention and concentration, and restlessness. In such cases it is very important to seek help from experts, as inappropriate use of most ADHD medications for GAD can worsen anxiety. GAD very commonly leads to depression as a comorbid condition. I rarely see people with chronic GAD who are not also depressed. GAD might run in the family, suggesting genetic susceptibility. Like social anxiety, aside from the genetic aspect, people can learn from parents that the world is not a safe place, and that they need to worry.

Brain imaging studies suggest increased amygdala and reduced prefrontal cortex activity in GAD.

OBSESSIVE-COMPULSIVE DISORDER

The most recent version of *DSM* has removed obsessive-compulsive disorder (OCD) from the category of anxiety disorders for scientific reasons outside the scope of this book. But I will address OCD in this chapter as anxiety is the major aspect of this illness. The hallmark of OCD is chronic presence of obsessions and/or compulsions. In psychiatry, an obsession is defined differently than in pop culture. Obsessions are recurrent, persistent, and intrusive unwanted thoughts, feelings, ideas, or images that are disturbing and hard to push away or ignore. The list of obsessions is infinite, but the common ones surround concerns of contamination, disorderliness, or asymmetry; checking for safety (did I turn off the stove?); profanity (intrusive curses or obscene images); unwanted thoughts of harming or having harmed others; or an urge to count or repeat numbers or words in a specific order or touch objects in a specific way.

Obsessions could be also very weird. This is not unusual in OCD and is not a sign of severe illness or psychosis. The patient knows the obsessions are illogical or extreme, and tries to avoid them, often with minimum success. For example, a patient may have intrusive unwanted thoughts that they might use a knife and hurt their family. Out of such fear, they will lock up all the sharp objects in a closet and give the key to their spouse.

For a better understanding of the obsession, here I will share some examples of what I have seen in my own clinic: One of my patients, whenever he was on the road, had a constant worry that he might have unknowingly run over someone. These thoughts were so concerning to him that he would drive back all the way, sometimes several times, to check and see if there was someone injured or dead on the roadside. This checking ritual took hours of his time every day. Another patient had intrusive unwanted images of his girlfriend having sex with her ex, every time he was having sex with her. I also saw a nun whose mind was rushed with curse words and obscene sexual images when sitting at the service. It should not be difficult for the reader to see how distressing and time consuming each of these obsessions could be when they continue for hours a day.

While obsessions are intrusive ideas, words, and images, compulsions are actions. A compulsion is a repeated ritualistic behavior that is often a reaction to an obsession. For example, when the obsession is about contamination, the compulsion is excessive washing or cleaning, handwashing, or bathing. I have had patients who, before treatment, spent several hours every day cleaning their home with sanitizer in a specific orderly ritual. Often they felt they did not do it in the right way or order, and had to restart the whole cleaning. They would at times wash their hands tens of times a day, and stay in the shower for hours. Some patients have to touch things in a special order; for example, if their hand touches something, it should be an odd number of times. One of my patients, a successful businessman, had to dial his car radio four stations to the left, three stations to the right, and two stations back to the left before being able to leave his car every time he parked, or something bad would happen. The same patient avoided walking on the handicapped parking lines. Although he logically knew none of this made sense, he could not convince his obsessions to stop.

OCD is less common than other fear-and-anxiety-related disorders and affects 1 percent of the population. Additionally, OCD is equally common among men and women. Depression is common in people with OCD, and there is some correlation between tic disorders (such as Tourette's) and OCD. Brain abnormalities in OCD are somewhat different from other anxiety disorders and involve basal ganglia, a part of the brain with an important role in planning actions and movement.

Like other disorders in this chapter, OCD is treatable, which I will explain in chapter 10.

ADJUSTMENT DISORDER WITH ANXIETY

Before we close this chapter, it is important to note that clinical anxiety is not always caused by internal factors or experiences of the past. Excessive anxiety is often a reaction to stressful events that are difficult to navigate. Adjustment disorder is a clinical condition where the emotional reaction to life's challenges is out of proportion and maladaptive, and impairs the person's ability to function. The events leading to adjustment disorder often include major life transitions such as loss of a loved one, getting married, getting a new job, having a new child, breakups, or financial challenges. While all these events are somewhat stressful to most people, in adjustment disorder, the anxiety is too much and beyond what an average person would experience.

Chapter 9

Haunting Memories

Trauma and PTSD

I have seen a couple burn alive in a car, I have seen a three-year-old fro-
zen outside, my partner was shot to death with a shotgun next to me. For
the past ten years I have had nightmares of shooting and chasing every
night, and flashbacks every day. There is not a day I do not think about
my partner.

—Tearful Detroit police officer

As our society is beginning to open its eyes to the long-lasting impact of trauma on people, the scientific community is also excelling in learning what trauma does to the human mind, brain, and body. Until recently, posttraumatic stress disorder (PTSD) was seen only as a disease of combat veterans. But thanks to research, advocacy efforts, and public education, now more people are aware of the extent of trauma exposure among different groups of people, and the hurts it can cause. On the other hand, public use of the words trauma and PTSD has become too loose; they have become a fad.

In this chapter I will explain trauma, what it does to the brain and the body, its impact in different populations and society at large, and childhood trauma and its long-term effects. I am especially excited about writing this chapter because this is a major area of my research and clinical expertise.

WHAT IS TRAUMA?

As the public and pop culture interest in trauma have increased (e.g., Google searches for the word "trauma" almost doubled between 2010 and 2022), its use has also become too casual. I have seen people address difficult experiences or any stressful life event like a divorce, job loss, breakup, move, loss of a loved one, or even a Twitter post as traumatic. Some use this term for any unfortunate, saddening, hurtful, or offending experience. Given what is known about the debilitating impact of trauma on people, this loose use of the terminology is not only a disservice to those really traumatized, but also disempowering to those who believe they are traumatized but are not. Furthermore, it opens the doors to quacks who hand words like PTSD or complex trauma like candies out to people, to sell their snake oil. I have in many instances told people who came to me for treatment of their "complex PTSD": "You do not have PTSD, and that is good news!" Of course I do not mean to minimize the stressful impact of tough life experiences, but not all of them are traumatic.

In psychiatry the word "trauma" has a precise definition and refers to very specific experiences. *DSM* defines trauma as "actual or threatened death, serious injury, or sexual violence." These experiences are horrific to all humans and can seriously threaten one's life or physical or emotional being. Traumatic events include but are not limited to war, terrorist attacks, shootings, torture, assault, robbery, physical abuse, rape and sexual violence, serious motor vehicle accidents, and natural disasters. Trauma does not impact us only by direct personal experience. Witnessing it happen to someone else (e.g., seeing someone shot or tortured), repeated exposure to details of others' trauma, or aftermath of a traumatic event can also traumatize the witnesses. I commonly see this type of trauma among war refugees, first responders, emergency medical staff, and veterans. For refugees and civilians who have been in war zones, even in the absence of personal experience, exposure to death, injuries, and torment of others is common. First responders like emergency personnel, firefighters, police officers, and dispatchers are regularly exposed to scenes and aftermaths of shootings, tragic deaths, domestic abuse, serious physical injury, fire, and other horrible events that they are the first to rush into. Trauma could also happen via direct exposure to details of traumatic experiences of loved ones or close friends, and repeated exposure to graphic details via media or work-related exposure (journalists or crime investigators).

Throughout this chapter, I will intentionally avoid disaster pornography and detailed description of the traumatic stories I have heard during my career as a trauma specialist. At the same time, I will try to portray an accurate picture of how people with such experiences are impacted, and how they try to deal with their pain. Trauma exposure is a lot more common that most might imagine; depending on different studies, up to 50 to 90 percent of US adults have experienced at least one traumatic event in their life. Exposure in children is also high especially in urban areas and poverty-stricken communities, and is too often underreported. Estimates suggest that nearly half of the children in the US have witnessed community violence, and one in ten have witnessed violence between parents or caregivers. Due to the complexities of collecting this kind of data and underreporting, it is hard to know exact extent of exposure, but most studies suggest one in five children having experienced sexual abuse, and a same number physical abuse. Trauma exposure is much higher among survivors of torture and human trafficking, refugees of war, combat veterans, first responders, and emergency personnel. For example, in a 2013 study, more than 80 percent of the police officers surveyed reported having seen dead bodies and severely assaulted people over the past year.

IMPACT OF TRAUMA EXPOSURE

While most people might consider PTSD as its only outcome, trauma can cause a variety of, and different degrees of, physical and mental health problems. Immediately after trauma, survivors can have different reactions ranging from emotional detachment, confusion, sadness, numbness, fear, anxiety, panic, insomnia, feeling on edge, agitation, nightmares, poor concentration, or hopelessness, as well as physical symptoms of pain, hyperventilation, stomach upset, rapid heart rate, sweating, or headaches. These common reactions that can last for days are not necessarily abnormal. During the dangerous experience, the fight-or-flight system is activated, and it takes some time to slow down. Seeking professional help at this stage helps in screening for warning signs and ensuring safe and healthy recovery. Those who know the survivors can offer support and care in a safe environment. It is important to resist the urge to push the person to share details of their experience, which could negatively impact both the survivor and the listener (via vicarious exposure). It is most helpful to help them feel safe, give them food or a glass of water or some tea, give them space and control, and listen to them if they need to talk.

For most people, these symptoms gradually or quickly subside, and they can return to their normal life. I remember I saw a young police officer who heroically helped her partner who was shot, a few days after the incident. She was feeling nervous and found it difficult to sleep. I gave her some lifestyle recommendations and asked to see her in a couple of weeks, when she was already back to normal life. She still often thought of her lost partner, which was normal mourning. Like mourning, each trauma-exposed person may recover at their own pace. This can depend on the trauma intensity and type, and the unique nature of each person and their environment. For some people, symptoms may continue or even progress. For others, symptoms may have delayed onset and not show up for a relatively long time.

In the long term, trauma can cause a variety of mental and physical issues. Anxiety and depression are very common outcomes. In our research at STARC funded by the National Institute of Child Health and Human Development (NICHD), in Syrian and Iraqi refugees of war who had resettled in the US, 40 percent of men and one in two women were highly anxious, even two years after having left their home country. In the same study we found clinical depression affecting half of the refugees (again more common among women). Half of the children were highly anxious, and two-thirds of them experienced separation anxiety. That is because when a child has seen extreme violence and danger, the most adaptive reaction would be to stick close to the parents and not leave their side, in order to remain safe. But unfortunately, trauma causes this learned behavior to linger even after one has left the dangerous environment. Substance use, often to self-medicate the mental agony, and anger and irritability are other common outcomes.

POSTTRAUMATIC STRESS DISORDER

PTSD is probably the only psychiatric condition that needs an external event: trauma. Without history of trauma, PTSD does not happen. *DSM*'s first criterion (A) for PTSD requires direct or indirect experience of traumatic event(s) as defined earlier. PTSD is basically an unhinged chronic switch to the fight-or-flight mode in the brain and the body, even years after the trauma. The brain constantly screens for danger, and forces the person to avoid any situation slightly reminding them of or resembling the painful experience. *DSM* clusters PTSD symptoms in four categories:

Hyperarousal symptoms happen because of a switch to constant alertness and screening for any potential threat. Hyperarousal manifests itself in the form of hypervigilance, being easily startled, hyperfocused attention on any sign of unsafety, poor concentration, and insomnia. The mind is watching day and night for any sign that might suggest something dangerous is about to happen. I have had veterans with PTSD who could not leave their gun, even when going to the bathroom. I see firefighters and cops who can only go to a restaurant with their family if it is not a busy time, and they sit next to the exit with their back to the wall where they can see everything. When they enter a building, the first thing they check automatically is the exits. Most people with PTSD avoid crowds because it is difficult to watch for danger when there are too many things and people to scan. Some even become homebound and do not want to be outside where the bad thing might happen. I once worked with a survivor of sexual assault who would get so anxious around people that she was even doing her grocery shopping online. Constantly being on edge can also lead to short temper, irritability, and anger.

Avoidance: Traumatic experiences are so painful that the survivors tend to avoid anything reminding them of their trauma. They try to avoid the memories of trauma and anything that reminds them of those memories. For example, some first responders and reporters who have been at the scenes of tragedies find reexposure to the story and images of the event through media and social media, or curious friends and neighbors, painful. Some even hide their occupation in the fear that people at a party may ask them about the recent school shooting they responded to. For refugees and veterans, reports or stories of war in their or other countries, or war-related movies, are bothersome.

People with PTSD may also avoid places that are in some way associated with where the trauma happened. One of my patients who was robbed at a gas station avoided going to gas stations, or parking structures alone. The time of trauma also plays a role in avoidance. A lot of times people feel nervous around the time of the day it happened, or the days before its anniversary. Some people even make major life changes to avoid the reminders. I had a patient who was raped by a classmate in the first year of college. The next day she left that town and that college, and never went back again. In her sixties, she still avoided anything that reminded her of that town. Survivors of rape often find it difficult to be around men or people resembling the perpetrator. One of my patients, a rape survivor, was terrified and could not sleep for weeks ahead of a court date where she would have to recall the event and— worse—possibly face the perpetrator. This avoidance is actually a common reason rape survivors hesitate to take legal action against their predators. There are organizations and advocacy groups that focus their mission on preparing these people for what will happen in court. Veterans and survivors of shootings usually avoid war movies that are too realistic (e.g., some may like war movies, but *Saving Private Ryan* is too much).

Intrusion symptoms include flashbacks, frequent nightmares, and recurrent intrusive memories of the trauma. Nightmares disrupt sleep, and some dread sleeping because they are worried about the nightmares they will have. Nightmares could be repetition of the event, or totally irrelevant to it. A survivor of a shooting can dream of being shot at, shooting others, failing to save someone, being chased, or dying. Flashbacks are perceptual reexperience of the trauma as if it is happening in the here and now. For example, after hearing a loud noise resembling an explosion, a veteran or a war refugee begins to see the scenes of combat; hear the sounds of weapons, helicopters, and explosions; and smell burning rubber or flesh. Olfactory flashbacks can be triggered by any remotely relevant smell. Survivors of rape often have flashbacks of the body smell or perfume of the perpetrator, or feel their touch on their body. Memories of trauma, triggered or untriggered, keep haunting the person, and are commonly accompanied by anxiety, guilt, shame, and sadness.

Negative mood and thinking: Trauma changes one's worldview, sense of self, and memories. They might forget important parts of an event or lose interest in life and not find joy in the activities they used to enjoy. They can feel emotionally detached from the outside world, loved ones, and even themselves. Feelings of guilt and shame and seeing the world as a brutal, unfair, and unfriendly place are also common. Survivor's guilt is horrible. A veteran might think for years about why he survived when his friends did not, and even avoid anything joyful because his dead comrades are not able to enjoy it. I have seen firefighters, cops, and EMTs who for years were plagued with wondering if there was something else they could have done to save the teenager who overdosed. Survivors of rape, abuse, and torture commonly feel ashamed, damaged, and incomplete. I spend a great deal of our time in treatment helping patients fight these maladaptive and inaccurate thoughts and feelings.

For an official diagnosis of PTSD, besides the experience of trauma, *DSM* requires at least one of the intrusion and avoidance symptoms, and two of the hyperarousal and negative mood and cognition symptoms. As I explained before, this does not mean that those who miss a criterion are not impacted or do not need help. What we really care about in the clinic is the distress and dysfunction caused by the symptoms. For diagnosing PTSD, the symptoms should have existed for more than a month; before that, it is technically called "acute stress disorder." This is important to know, as for some people, the symptoms resolve over the first month and do not continue to PTSD.

Trauma is very common, and so is PTSD. Full-blown PTSD affects nearly 8 percent of the US population at some point in their life and is more common in women. It is highly accompanied by depression, anxiety, substance use, and physical pain. I have rarely seen a patient with chronic PTSD who did not also have depression. When I see trauma and substance use together, I always ask, "Some dance to remember, some dance to forget. Why do you use?" This helps me detect the most disturbing symptoms they are trying to self-medicate with drugs, so I can address them with safer medications or therapy. By the way, I hope you got the "Hotel California" reference.

Trauma that is perpetrated by humans, such as torture, rape, assault, and abuse, is more likely to cause PTSD, compared to, say, natural disasters. This could be because we are specifically sensitive to the pain perpetrated by our own species, compared to what comes from the outside world.

TRAUMA AND RESILIENCE

Not all those who experience trauma develop PTSD. Some people have symptoms temporarily, and some do not have any. There are a variety of biological, psychological, and environmental factors that together determine who will or will not be impacted. Severity of trauma, its source (humans or nature), recurrence, genetic and epigenetic buildup, personal meaning of trauma, past experiences, poverty and other concurrent stressors, environmental support and care, and many other known and unknown factors decide the impact. Therefore, we can never know for sure who will develop PTSD after exposure, although we are beginning to research common aspects of risk and resilience. To fight stigma, the public needs to know this and avoid judgment, guilt, shame, or feeling weak for those who do develop PTSD or other mental impacts of trauma.

While most of the research has been on risk and vulnerability, there is now important research happening on resilience to trauma impact. This covers both internal (biology, past, beliefs, meaning) and external (support, family, environment) factors. For example, at STARC we have found that those refugee children whose parents are less stressed by their own anxiety and PTSD, as well as environmental issues like finances, housing, and government support, recover faster after having left the war zone.

Some people even become stronger after trauma and grow and develop a deeper sense of purpose, themselves, life and its meaning, and what matters most. For them, trauma puts in perspective what is and what is not important in life, and washes away the illusions. Some turn their pain, anger, and frustration into action, and dedicate their time to prevent trauma in their fellow humans. Some become social workers, therapists, first responders, doctors, trauma researchers, or social activists. Some may run for office to advocate for policy changes to mitigate childhood trauma or mass shootings.

TRAUMA IN SPECIAL POPULATIONS

I drove with a mother and her seven-year-old and eight-month-old baby. They had been outside in freezing temperature for forty-eight hours. The mom told me she had to put the baby inside their luggage for the night when it was coldest. But during the night she saw how the baby of another family who stayed outside died since they didn't have luggage or anything else to put her in to stay warm.

—Finnish driver transporting Ukrainian refugees across the border

Some groups of people are much more likely to experience trauma and also have repeated exposure. Ongoing trauma and stress not only increase the impact by exhausting the brain and the body, but also curtail recovery. Because PTSD was first noticed in combat veterans, we know more about it in this population. Depending on the level of exposure, 11 to 30 percent of US combat-exposed veterans meet the criteria for PTSD at some point in their life.

Other groups are urban civilians especially in poverty-stricken areas, where ongoing life stress complicates the picture and may limit the ability to cope and recover. Survivors of human trafficking endure years of manipulation, trauma, threats to life, and sexual violence. When removed from the environment of abuse, they have to work hard to build a new life while facing socioeconomic challenges and their trauma-related symptoms.

War and ongoing conflicts around the world continue to create refugee crises and displacement of about 1 percent of the world's population. Refugees and internally displaced people experience enormous trauma and stress. They are untrained civilians unequipped for self-defense, with long exposure to military trauma (bombings and explosions; gore scenes of death, mutilation, and torture; kidnapping and harassment). For a soldier who goes to war, training and preparation, being armed, and affiliation to an army all provide some protection and a sense of control and agency that refugees do not have. Refugees also endure months and years of uncertainty, lack of access to basic resources, exposure to death and suffering of others, fear of harm to themselves and their families, hunger, and lack of shelter. Those who are lucky enough, leave behind their loved ones—dead or alive—their homes, jobs, culture, memories, and more, to flee to overly crowded refugee camps. They often stay in these camps for several years before being sent to a country where they have to navigate a whole new way of life and deal with poverty, cultural and language differences, unemployment, and prejudices. These countless and chronic stressors complicate consequences of trauma for refugees.

Prevalence of mental health issues caused by trauma is very high among refugees. In our study of the impact of war trauma on Syrian and Iraqi refugees resettling in the state of Michigan, we found that one in three refugees met the criteria for PTSD, two years after having left their home country. For some, including those who were tortured, the prevalence is as high as 80 percent. Refugees also suffer a very high level of comorbid anxiety and depression, as high as 50 percent in our research cohort in Michigan.

Although some people might think that leaving the environment of trauma will remove the impact, research suggests otherwise. In our study, we followed up with our refugees two years after the initial visit (now four years since they left Syria). We failed to find a significant decline in the symptoms of PTSD, anxiety, and depression. For the survivors of physical or sexual assault or torture, PTSD symptoms even worsened over time. Clinical experience supports these research findings. In my clinic I have seen people who were assaulted, robbed, shot at, or raped many years ago, and still had symptoms of PTSD. The Detroit police officer I quoted in the beginning of this chapter had been suffering from nightmares and flashback every day and night for a decade, before coming to my clinic.

First responders, including police officers, firefighters, emergency medical personnel, and dispatchers, are another group with regular exposure to the worst of what humans suffer, or do to each other. Over the years I have worked with many of them and have found their stories the toughest to hear. Long work hours interfere with family activities and routines, sleep is all over the place, and they often feel not understood by their loved ones and society. Decisions are made in split seconds in life-and-death situations that affect the lives of themselves, their colleagues, and people they serve, and their career. I have heard countless times from EMTs, police, and firefighters that they still think about what they could had done differently many years ago, so that infant or their partner would still be alive.

Once I was at a fire station for a ride-along. I did the ride-alongs to help me understand the first responders and their challenges better before trying to help them in the clinic. Firefighters have a tradition that every day one of them cooks for the whole team, and they are usually great cooks! I grabbed a plate and was sitting at the table waiting for others to join before I started eating. The firefighter sitting next to me was already eating. Surprised that I was waiting, he said, "If you do not eat *now*, you might not be able to finish your food." He was right—shortly after I took my first bite, we were in the truck, riding to the scene of an accident! A first responder's job requires very quick shifts in both pace and task, switching from watching a game on the couch at the fire station, to driving fast to a fire scene a couple minutes later, and pulling injured people out of a burning car an hour later. A police officer might be at the scene of a car accident at one moment, investigating a domestic abuse case ten minutes later, resuscitating an infant in front of her terrified family two hours later, and trying to help fix a family dispute later in the day. Some calls are random and unnecessary. Once on a ride-along, I even saw a woman who called the police to ask them not to allow her husband in their house, because she was planning to file for divorce!

An officer once told me, "When I pull someone over, to them I am an annoyance. To me, there might be a gun on the other side of the window." A first responder's job inherently involves risk of serious harm to the person and their colleagues. Every time they go on a call, there is possibility of injury. One of my firefighter patients was trapped under a blazing roof that collapsed on him for several minutes before he was rescued. He sustained third-degree burns and dealt with PTSD for years after the incident. I had a twenty-two-year-old police officer who lost her partner and close friend to a shooting right next to her, and still remembers his blood staining the seats of her car.

A group whose trauma exposure is often unknown to the public is the dispatchers. Although they sit in an office physically away from the trauma, they hear the details of horrible events on the emergency calls and from the first responders. Their work is very fast paced, transitioning from one traumatic call to another, and involves tough decisions on prioritizing and routing the calls. They might hear a child describe the bloody view of his murdered family, or receive a call from a victim of abuse whose life was threatened. After guiding the message to the appropriate first responders, they rarely know what happened, and if the persons involved survived.

As mentioned earlier in this chapter, in a recent study, 80 percent of police officers reported having seen dead bodies or victims of assault over the past year. PTSD is common and affects about 20 percent of first responders. Many others experience subthreshold symptoms of PTSD and anxiety like insomnia and flashbacks, and some cope through excessive drinking. Suicide is too common among first responders also. Ongoing stress and trauma complicate recovery once they develop PTSD.

While a first responder's job involves trauma exposure on a regular basis, what is the one incident that flares the PTSD? I have seen some of them who were functioning well for decades all of a sudden be devastated by death of a child. I have contemplated this question and have found that personal connection is a possible player. For example, one of my firefighters began to experience PTSD right after seeing a child the age of his own son die from overdose. Another reached the breaking point when he lost his partner, and another after a run to a shooting at her own child's school. I will further discuss this personal connection to trauma in chapter 12.

WHAT TRAUMA DOES TO THE BRAIN

Neuroimaging research suggests increased activation in brain areas involved in generation and experience of fear and anxiety (amygdala and insula) and impaired architecture and function in emotion regulation areas (hippocampus and frontal cortical regions). There is also a sensitization to reminders of trauma. A few years ago, we reviewed studies of electroencephalography (EEG; brain waves) in PTSD. We found that the automatic brain responses and brain waves indicative of attention were stronger in response to any image or sound that was related to trauma or suggested danger (explosion, angry face). This was paired with a reduced response to neutral cues (image of a plant). Similarly, brain imaging studies show increased amygdala and insula response to trauma-related images and sounds, angry or fearful faces, or other negative stimuli.

Studies have found that not only can PTSD lead to decreased volume and function of the hippocampus, but also a smaller hippocampus is a vulnerability factor to developing PTSD in response to trauma. For example, researchers looked at the size of the hippocampus in identical twins of patients with

PTSD, and found those identical twins also had a smaller hippocampus. The smaller the hippocampus was in one twin, their combat-exposed veteran twin was more likely to develop PTSD symptoms. This points to a very interesting interaction between biology (nature), and the environment (nurture) in brain response to trauma. Chronic and untreated PTSD can worsen the brain changes over time, suggesting that untreated PTSD might become a progressive illness.

People have asked me about use of brain scans in diagnosing PTSD, as some places claim to do it (at a hefty cost). The clear, undoubted answer is: "*No*, do not waste your time and money." And I say this as an expert in brain imaging research and PTSD. While we use brain imaging for researching average changes in the brains of large groups of people with PTSD, or for that matter, any psychiatric disorder, we are not at the stage of science and technology to use brain scans for making clinical diagnoses. The only current way to diagnose PTSD and anxiety disorders is clinical interviews and observations.

We have also been learning about genetic and epigenetic vulnerability to PTSD. There are ongoing international efforts to combine genetic data from tens of thousands of people from across the globe, which will enable us to examine genetic variations that might make some more vulnerable. Genetic differences in processing serotonin, dopamine, norepinephrine, and stress hormones are some candidates. Epigenetic changes (change in expression of genes due to environment impact) can increase vulnerability in not only the person, but also in their offspring, and explain part of the intergenerational transmission of trauma. My colleague Dr. Dalia Khalil and I are currently researching how epigenetic changes in a refugee mother might impact their child who is born in the US after migration, and never saw the war.

WHAT TRAUMA DOES TO THE BODY

Chronic exposure to stress and trauma and the stress response triggered by PTSD all have long-term negative impacts on the body. There is cumulative evidence suggesting that both childhood trauma and untreated PTSD can increase heart disease, high blood pressure, diabetes, obesity, chronic pain, and other medical conditions.

Inflammation might also play a role in PTSD, at least in some people. As I mentioned in chapter 3, during a stress response, inflammatory reactions prepare the body for recovery and fighting infections. But a chronic activation of this system due to PTSD can have a determinantal impact on the body. Not only are inflammatory molecules higher in some patients with PTSD, but also, studies suggest active inflammation throughout the adult life in people who have endured trauma and adverse events in their childhood. Expression of genes involved in inflammatory response is also linked with PTSD, and adverse and traumatic experiences can activate these genes. Chronic exposure to inflammation could be responsible for some of the long-term bodily diseases that are more common in PTSD. If these research findings continue to replicate, at some point in the future we might begin to treat PTSD with anti-inflammatory medications in some patients.

Chronic hyperactivity of the sympathetic nervous system is an integral part of PTSD, as the PTSD brain is always in a state of threat detection and overly prepared for fight or flight. The consequences of this sympathetic hyperactivity are insomnia and nightmares, jitteriness, increased heart rate, and high blood pressure. Research by my colleagues shows that increased sympathetic activation right after trauma can actually predict a higher likelihood of developing PTSD. At the STARC lab, we collected skin conductance responses when children were telling us about their traumatic experiences. We found that in these children, sympathetic responses to trauma memories were associated with reexperience and hyperarousal symptoms of PTSD. The higher the sympathetic activity during these interviews, the larger the PTSD symptoms. These findings are fascinating as they might help us at some point in the future in predicting who might have a higher likelihood of developing PTSD, right after trauma exposure. A chronic hyperactive sympathetic state puts too much pressure on the cardiovascular system, causing heart disease, high blood pressure, and diabetes.

CHILDHOOD TRAUMA

Unfortunately, trauma exposure is too common among children and adolescents, and in many cases, it is repeated. Violence, bullying, and physical and sexual abuse are common, and often underreported. In my clinic, I have repeatedly heard from adults about their childhood experience of sexual abuse, and often I was the only one who learned about their trauma so many years later. In many cases, adults and caregivers ignored or did not believe their reports. These unfortunate experiences are usually very confusing to children, and fear, shame, and guilt may prevent them from even talking about them. It is hard for the kids to understand why adults who are supposed to protect them would abuse them. Like in adults, childhood trauma can lead to PTSD, anxiety, depression, poor school performance, and substance use in children. Unfortunately, childhood traumatic experiences can have lingering, lifelong effects. In the long term, unaddressed childhood trauma—even when not causing PTSD during childhood—can increase the risk of PTSD, anxiety, depression, substance use, suicide, pain, and a variety of medical conditions like high blood pressure, diabetes, and obesity in adulthood. Early intervention is critical in preventing long-lasting effects on the person's mental and physical health and prosperity.

WHAT TRAUMA DOES TO THE COMMUNITIES

Collective trauma impacts communities and nations. In the more obvious form, war, occupation, and oppression affect nations for generations, via cultural and epigenetic changes, and intergenerational transmission of trauma. People of a country will find it hard to trust the outsiders, will be too cautious and worried about resources and possible loss; they will not be able to relax. Culturally, they can lose their ability for joy because of too much focus on what could go wrong and possible threats. As discussed in chapter 7, negative cycles of aggression and violence could be a result of large-scale trauma exposure.

Another large-scale trauma is what sadly happens too often in America: mass shooting tragedies. These events take too many lives and devastate not only the victims, first responders, and the communities where they happen, but also the nation at large. Every time a shooting happens in a new place (a school, a movie theater, a grocery store, a concert), that place is no longer on the list of safe places in people's minds. As school shootings keep happening, more parents worry about their children; we see this so often in the clinic. When at a movie or a restaurant, some people automatically check the exits and envision a survival plan in case a shooting happens. Some decide to avoid public events completely. Frequent exposure to the news and images can create a feeling that they are too probable. Younger children might even think that they are happening nearby. When seeing repeated coverage of the same event on the news, they might think each report is an independent shooting. Research shows that exposure to the news of mass shootings and terrorist events can cause not only high anxiety, but also PTSD symptoms in people who were not there when the event happened. In chapter 15 I will talk more about how news media exposure scares society at large. Sadly for some people, such frequent exposure can lead to a feeling of helplessness, desensitization, and numbness to tragedies, and accepting them as the new norm.

Chapter 10

Taming the Beast

How Clinicians Treat Fear and Anxiety

The best way out is always through.

—Robert Frost, American poet

WE HAVE COME A LONG WAY

Over the past century, Western psychiatric treatments of fear and anxiety have evolved from terrifying approaches like submerging people in cold water or institutionalizing people with severe OCD, to mostly outpatient effective treatments. But psychiatric approaches in the East seem to have older roots. One of the old records of treating mental illness is about the work of Iranian physician Ibn e Sina (famously known as Avicenna). The story tells about a prince who had stopped eating, and had a delusion that he was a cow. He kept begging to be butchered so that "a good stew may be made from my flesh." After examining the patient, Ibn e Sina said in front of the patient, "What a lean cow he is; he should be fed before he is ready to be butchered." The prince eagerly ate not only the nutritious food every day, but also the medicines that were put in it, and recovered in a month's time.

But the beginning of psychiatry as a science is marked by Freud's theory of mind. Freud addressed anxiety as neurosis, and a result of conflict between the conscious and unconscious aspects of the mind, mostly rooted in childhood experiences and parenting. Consequently, psychoanalytic treatment aimed to resolve the unconscious conflicts by analyzing a patient's dreams, or by use of free associations: an uncensored, effortless flow of thoughts. In trying to find the roots of current fears in childhood, a patient's fear of dogs

101

could be tracked to an angry dad who yelled too often. The fear of dogs was then interpreted as a symbolic reaction to the father. Although treatments based on psychoanalytic theory are still being used, they have evolved away from a strict approach of interpreting everything as a result of unconscious conflict caused by parents.

Recent advances in neuroscience and our understanding of fear mechanisms in the brain and the body have led to a leap in appearance of more evidence-based, effective, and safe treatment methods. A deep coverage of all treatments of fear and anxiety would require multiple volumes. But the aim of this chapter is to familiarize the reader with the mainstream evidence-based treatments, exciting cutting-edge innovations, and how to navigate the healthcare system for those who might need evaluation and treatment.

AVAILABLE TREATMENTS

I have learned over the years that when one's mind is made up, this diminishes fear; knowing what must be done does away with fear.

—Rosa Parks

Most currently available treatments fall within two categories: psychotherapies and medications. Psychotherapy, or the talking cure, happens within the context of working with a therapist to explore the origins and nature of fears, anxieties, and maladaptive behaviors. Then the therapist will help the patient to modify less adaptive behaviors and distorted perception of self, others, and the world, which leads to reduction of anxiety.

Medications are used to reduce the mental and physical intensity of anxiety by adjusting the levels and functions of brain neurotransmitters. Most of these medications do not add anything new to the brain chemistry, they just adjust the level of the brain's own chemicals.

In recent years, the use of technology has broadened horizons in treatment of anxiety. Some of these methods include modulating brain activity by electromagnetic fields, and employing virtual and augmented reality to help people face their fears.

PSYCHOTHERAPY

The beginning of modern psychotherapy involved psychoanalysis, an intense and very long therapy method, requiring several sessions a week of treatment for years. With the complexities of modern life, economic considerations, and busy schedules, however, even if effective, this method is not very realistic and can only be afforded by a small number of people.

Since Freud, others have revised and improved his theories, and today's psychodynamic psychotherapy (psychotherapy based on psychoanalytic theories) is different than what was done by Freud. It is usually shorter and does not require lying on the couch five days a week for years to resolve a phobia.

Like most of our bodily functions including hearts, lungs, and the digestive system are automatic, unconscious, and barely under our voluntary control, psychoanalytic theories believe most of what our mind does is automatic and unconscious. The focus of psychoanalysis is on resolving the unconscious conflicts and maladaptive patterns, by bringing them to awareness. Psychodynamic therapies are based on the following principles:

a. *Transference* is a core aspect of psychoanalysis, the phenomenon through which the patient transfers feelings and emotions from the past to the here and now. For example, a patient who had a judgmental parent might have learned that authorities and superiors are all judgmental. The same feeling will be also projected onto the therapist, and then analyzed and discussed in therapy. Bringing the automatic transference to the light of conscious awareness leads to learning that the patient is not a defenseless, vulnerable child anymore. Transference analysis allows for a more objective understanding of the world based on the realities of the here and now, instead of the shadow of the past.

b. *Free association* is the process of allowing the mind to wander freely with one thought leading to another, without filtering them. Psychoanalytic theory asserts that this free flow of thoughts leads to emergence of the unconscious material, allowing the patient and the therapist to see how unconscious processes cause negative emotions.

c. *Dream interpretation:* Freud called dreams "the royal road to the unconscious" and viewed them as the symbolic language of the unconscious in expressing its fears, wishes, and conflicts. In this approach, characters and events in the dreams symbolize the unconscious thinking condensed into a timeless chaos. Disentangling the dreams provides the therapist and the patient with an opportunity to see the unconscious fears and anxieties in an unfiltered form.

d. *Defense mechanisms:* In psychoanalytic theory, defense mechanisms are unconscious mental processes that aim at reducing conflict and anxiety. For example, *denial defense* pushes the conflicts and negative emotions below the conscious awareness. Through *displacement*, people may displace their anger at their boss (which if expressed can cost them their job) onto their spouse or pet when they come home from work.

By analyzing the defenses, the patient gains insight into the anxiety and conflict that lie beneath them.

Among anxiety disorders, psychoanalysis is mostly used for treatment of generalized anxiety disorder.

COGNITIVE THERAPY

Cognitive therapy was developed by Aaron Beck, who was trained as a psychoanalyst. The foundation of cognitive therapy is that negative emotions are caused by maladaptive *automatic thoughts*, or *cognitive distortions*. For example, Joe might believe that unless he is liked by everybody, he is not good or worthy enough. This is accompanied by an automatic thought that unless others show constant positive attention, they do not like Joe. One morning at the office, a colleague is too busy and preoccupied to notice Joe, and Joe concludes that he is not likable. This conclusion, which might have been made at a subconscious and automatic level, causes anxiety and sadness. During cognitive therapy, the patient and the therapist will identify and examine the validity of these predispositions. For example, Joe recalls that he felt anxious right after running into his colleague. The therapist will challenge Joe on his theory about why his colleague behaved the way she did that day. For example, she might have not noticed Joe because she had an argument with her spouse that morning, or was too busy with work, or simply did not get enough sleep the night before. The core belief that one needs to be liked by everyone is also challenged in treatment.

Common cognitive distortions include catastrophizing (always expecting the worst possible outcome), overgeneralization (generalizing one negative experience to all cases: if she doesn't like me, nobody does), and mind reading (I know what she is thinking about me). The course of cognitive therapy is usually ten to twelve sessions. After that, the patient can use the skills they learned in therapy to navigate future challenges.

EXPOSURE THERAPY

During the interview of a child with contamination OCD, I found out that his mother also had OCD with obsessions of orderliness. For treatment they built an alliance: mother would encourage her son to avoid excessive handwashing, and the son took on a mission to make some mess around the house to help mom overcome her urge for excessive orderliness.

Exposure therapy, or behavior therapy, is an effective mainstream treatment for phobias, OCD, and PTSD. The core basis of exposure therapy is extinction learning. As we learned earlier, in phobias for some reason the primitive brain has associated a safe situation or object (a pet dog or heights) to danger. This illogical association often cannot be changed by logic and discourse, as the patient already knows their fear is baseless. Continuing to avoid only strengthens the fear, as the disease goes: you see, when you avoid it, nothing bad happens.

Exposure therapy aims at breaking this cycle by proving the phobic belief to be wrong. The therapist helps the patient to gradually feel comfortable in the presence of the feared situation. For example, a patient who is afraid of dogs starts with looking at pictures of small dogs, then videos; then they practice being safe in presence of a dog that is leashed ten yards away, then gradually get closer until they feel comfortable near that dog. In the case of social phobia, the patient does gradual exposure to strangers and increments of crowds. In OCD, patient practices touching the surfaces and resisting the urge to wash hands, or in what we call exposure and response prevention, avoids ruminating the obsessions. In PTSD, trauma memories are recalled repeatedly, until the brain learns that these memories themselves are not dangerous. Exposure therapy for PTSD also involves safe situations that are avoided because of trauma. For instance, for patients with PTSD who avoid social encounters, the exposure focuses on helping them feel safe around others. Exposure therapy usually works within a limited number of sessions (ten to twelve). Patients are encouraged to continue exposure practices to prevent relapse of their fears.

Although exposure therapy is very effective, its use is limited by lack of access to feared situations or objects in the clinic. For example, most therapists do not have a dog or a snake or a spider, or a group of people (for social phobia) in their office to use for exposure therapy. That is why they often resort to using imaginal exposure, pictures, and videos. Later in this chapter I'll tell you about the exciting new virtual and augmented reality technologies that are developed to overcome this limitation.

Often cognitive and behavioral therapy are used together (CBT). For a patient with social phobia, while cognitive therapy addresses the distorted thinking that everybody is out there to judge and criticize the patient, exposure therapy allows practicing safety around the crowd.

MINDFULNESS-BASED THERAPY

—*Where are you?*
—*Here.*

—What time is it?
—Now.
—What are you?
—This moment.
—Dan Millman, *Way of the Peaceful Warrior*

A great advantage of the human mind is its ability to reflect on the past and plan for the future. But unfortunately, this asset has also become one of our biggest weaknesses, and a source of suffering for our species. Even as you are reading this sentence, a part of you is not here, and is wandering elsewhere. Our minds always wander in the past or worry about the future, while we miss the only reality: this moment; the only *real* moment in our life is right now. A second before and a second after now are both just the result of neural activities in our brain. The past, and the future, do not exist outside of our memory and imagination. If we were able to be fully present in the moment, most times we would not have a reason to worry. Based in the Eastern phi-losophies, the core principle of mindfulness practice is training our mind to bring its attention to the here and now. Leashing the wild monkey of the mind happens by using our senses to stay here. This can be done by focusing on our bodily sensations including our breathing or the sensory stimuli in our environment.

Let us do a two-minute experiment right now. Carefully look around you, and see how many colors you can count in your environment; really focus and see if you can find more colors. Try to also listen carefully and see how many sounds you can hear in your environment. Pay closer attention and see if you can identify more subtle sounds. Now, feel your clothes on your shoulders, every inch that touches your skin. If you are wearing shoes or socks, try to feel every inch of them. There are parts that feel less comfortable, and parts of your feet that do not even touch the shoes or the socks. Try to feel the texture of your shirt and describe it in detail.

Now, how much did you think about your worries of the past and the future during this experiment? This is mindfulness.

ART AND BODY-BASED THERAPY

Dance and movement therapy (DMT) focuses on the strong connection between the body and the brain, and the fact that our physical and mental sensations are intertwined. DMT and art therapy allow expression of difficult emotions through the body or the work of art. These are mindful activities with specific focus on breathing, bodily sensations, and expressive art. They are group based and promote creative ways of regulating negative emotions.

I became more familiar with these methods with the help of my friend and colleague Dr. Holly Feen-Calligan, who is an art therapist, and my former mentee and now colleague, Dr. Lana Grasser, who led our DMT research studies. Our team uses art therapy and DMT to help refugee children overcome their anxiety, a program that is used across the state of Michigan. Our research has found these low-cost interventions effective, and children love participating in them and continue to use them at home. During the pandemic, we even used these interventions remotely with the kids who joined the groups from their homes.

EXERCISE

Like most other physicians, recommending an active lifestyle to my patients was just a doctor chore for me until I saw its profound effects on my own mental and physical health. On a gloomy, snowy January night, a friend dragged me to a fitness boxing gym. I thought spending an hour punching a heavy bag was a stupid idea, but I was wrong. That day I barely survived the one hour of bag practice, but then I could not stop doing it. Having felt its impact with my own flesh and mind, I now convince my patients to commit to some degree of exercise, and we explore the options to see what physical activity works best for them. Interestingly, most of them love it and continue to be active when they see the effects for themselves.

Regular physical activity, especially cardio exercise, has proven to benefit brain health and cause growth in emotion regulation areas like the hippocampus. Exercise increases brain growth factors and reduces inflammation in the brain and the body. Regular exercise reduces the baseline heart rate, signaling a calmer internal environment to the brain. It also works like exposure therapy to physical symptoms of anxiety like fast-beating heart, hyperventilation, and sweatiness. Clinical studies have found regular cardio helpful in reduction of anxiety and depressive symptoms.

I teach my patients to see exercise as part of their treatment plan, a prescription: you take the pills that I prescribe for you; also take your exercise pill. It is one of the best investment someone can do: investing in their own body!

If you are interested in giving an active lifestyle a try, here are some quick tips:

- Pick something you can like, something that can become a hobby. What works for one does not necessarily work for another. For example, I hate running and treadmills, so if I wanted to insist on doing them, I would fail.

- Use positive peer pressure. My friends and I use a group app and tell each other when we plan to go to the gym.
- Do not see it as all or none. Exercise does not necessarily have to be one hour of driving to the gym, one hour spent at the gym, and one hour driving back, versus spending all those hours on the couch. If you are busy or tired from work, do less. I always say: five pushups are better than none, and each additional step is progress. You can even mix it with other activities: when talking on the phone, walk.
- When hesitating, ask yourself: "When was the last time I regretted doing it?"
- Finally, remember that exercise is not for weight loss, diet is. Many people give up on working out when they do not see great weight loss. You work out for your mental health, and the health of your heart, arteries, lungs, and joints.

MEDICATIONS

We have safe and effective medications for treatment of anxiety. They mostly work by reducing the mental and physical tone of the anxiety. As we have learned before, our attention, emotions, and thoughts are all intertwined and affect each other. The same way cognitive therapy reduces anxiety by correcting anxiety-inducing thoughts, by reducing the basic anxious tone in the body, medications help us to think more realistic and logically, and our attention to be less focused on anxiety-related cues in the environment.

The main class of medications used for treatment of anxiety is traditionally called "antidepressants." Despite the name, they are also used for treatment of anxiety, OCD, and PTSD. These medications are mostly from the family of *selective serotonin reuptake inhibitors* or SSRIs. SSRIs increase the availability of serotonin in the synapses by reducing its reabsorption, although we still do not have a clear idea about how exactly they reduce anxiety. Fluoxetine, sertraline, and paroxetine are some of these medications. Another group is *serotonin norepinephrine reuptake inhibitors* or SNRIs, which increase both serotonin and norepinephrine in the synaptic space between the neurons. Duloxetine and venlafaxine are examples of SNRIs. Antidepressant medications might take a few weeks at the needed dose to take effect. So, if you did not notice significant improvement after a few days, do not be disappointed. Sometimes we have to try a few antidepressants before we find the one that works best for each person, without causing side effects. It is important to address the stigma around these medications: when used judiciously and at the right dose and for the right indication, these medications are not addictive and do not change the person, or the way they think. They just reduce the intense anxiety, so the person can think and behave more logically, free from the effects of the unnecessary worries. Also, we have so many medications available, and people do not have to suffer the side effects; we can switch to another medication that does not have as many side effects for each person.

Benzodiazepines reduce anxiety by suppressing some of the brain neurons. Commonly used benzodiazepines are clonazepam, lorazepam, and alprazolam (famously known as Xanax). These medications should be used with caution as they can be addictive, and their long-term use might lead to memory impairment. That is why they are usually only used for short-term or situational anxiety. For example, if someone is afraid of flying and they only travel once a year, then I prescribe a small supply of lorazepam for them to use before their flight.

While medications mostly only work for as long as they are taken, effects of psychotherapy can be more enduring as they lead to resolution of conflicts and learning skills that can be used indefinitely after termination of therapy. That is why experts in anxiety disorders often recommend the use of medications in conjunction with therapy. I would also like to remind the readers to avoid use of medications without consulting with skilled physicians. That will prevent misdiagnosis and unnecessary and potentially harmful use of the medications.

Readers might have heard about the research studies on ketamine, cannabinoids, and psychedelics for severe treatment-resistant PTSD. We still need more data before we can comfortably use these agents as mainstream treatments. It is also important to know they can be addictive or cause serious harm in the wrong hands. For example, there is evidence from recent research that MDMA (a psychoactive drug) might help in specific psychotherapies of treatment-resistant PTSD. However, its use by unskilled people can cause more harm as the negative memories risen during the experiment must be handled by a trained psychotherapist.

On the cutting edge of neuroscience, there are also debates about possibility of changing—or even erasing—fear memories. Some studies have found that when a memory is recalled, it is malleable to change or modification. For example, researchers found that injection of an agent called anisomycin to a rat's amygdala within two weeks after fear conditioning could erase the fear memory via the process of *memory reconsolidation*! Despite this fascinating research on attempting to *erase* fear memories, the findings are still limited to the laboratory. There is a difference between a single sound or shape being associated in a rat brain with a foot shock, and repeated complex traumatic experiences consolidated over decades in a human PTSD brain. If this line of research succeeds, however, it will also raise the important moral and ethical dilemmas about erasing people's memories, or bringing the movie *Eternal Sunshine of the Spotless Mind* to reality.

NOVEL TECHNOLOGIES

Transcranial magnetic stimulation (TMS) is a noninvasive method that uses a magnetic field for stimulating the neurons near the surface of the brain. This is done by holding a magnetic coil near the patient's head. During the procedure the patient is awake and alert and does not even feel the procedure. TMS is used for treatment-resistant OCD and PTSD. *Deep brain stimulation*, or DBS, is used for treatment of severe and debilitating OCD. In this method, specific neurons are stimulated by surgical placement of electrodes in the brain by a neurosurgeon.

As noted earlier in this chapter, although exposure therapy is a very effective treatment, its use is limited by lack of access to feared objects or situations in the clinic. Over the past decade, virtual reality has been used to overcome this limitation: a patient with fear of heights can wear virtual reality goggles and find themselves on the top floor of a building. A patient with combat PTSD can see the streets of Iraq where they saw the explosion in the first place. A patient with fear of flying will sit in a virtual airplane ready to fly, and then take off, while the therapist is sitting next to them.

At STARC, I have invented a very exciting patented novel technology: *augmented reality* or AR exposure therapy. AR is the next wave of interactive human-computer technology that enables mixing virtual objects with physical reality. AR is different than VR in that it adds virtual objects to the real physical context (like in *Iron Man*). When the patient wears the AR goggles, the device maps their environment and provides the therapist with a 3D map of the surfaces surrounding them. The therapist can choose the feared objects (e.g., a spider or a dog) of different kinds and sizes (wolf, black widow, jumping spider; German shepherd, Doberman, pit bull) and place them in the patient's environment. The therapist can then command their behavior (the spider crawling from the floor to the wall to the ceiling; the dog walking, barking, or jumping).

Because AR allows the patients to see their real environment, they will be able to walk around and interact with objects, which creates an excellent sense of realism and control. In a clinical trial for fear of spiders, we found incredible efficacy: all patients who were initially terrified of spiders were able to touch a real live tarantula (Tony STARC), or the tank containing Tony in less than a one-hour therapy session!

After this discovery, and in a major leap in computer programming, we moved on to developing interactive human encounter scenarios to help patients overcome their social anxiety. Imagine standing in an empty room, where virtual humans of different sex, race, age, and body type gradually enter and fill the room, talking to each other or even coming and interacting with you, while your therapist is right there in the room.

Because the brain is in a constant state of threat detection, patients with PTSD find it very difficult to be around the crowd, which causes significant disability. That is why we also use AR technology for treatment of PTSD. We have even created police and fire station scenarios to help first responders with PTSD. While use of AR in PTSD is very novel and we are still research-ing the impact, the initial results are as amazing as the phobia treatment. One of the police officers I treated with this technology was so stressed by her trauma that she was even doing grocery shopping online. When we used the crowd AR scenario, she was standing in the corner of the room, with her arms crossed and back to the wall, where she could see all the virtual humans. Her subjective anxiety was 9 out of 10. One hour later, I left her alone in the room with fifteen virtual humans, and her anxiety was 2 out of 10. That night, she went to a game night!

This technology offers us boundless opportunities for helping people with PTSD, social anxiety, autism spectrum disorders, and even for skills training. A person can engage in a dating experience or a job interview with an AR avatar, or give a lecture to a group of AR humans. Or a police officer could walk around a neighborhood and interact with virtual humans of different behaviors or mental health backgrounds. At STARC, we are even beginning to combine this technology with artificial intelligence (AI). For example, based on the specific needs of a patient, I can write the character of an AR human, and the patient can have a conversation with that human, whose responses are generated by the AI! When combined with telemedicine, this technology can bring treatment to patients' homes, like treating fear of spiders in the patient's own basement or bedroom!

You can find a demo video of this technology on my lab website under "Projects": https://www.starclab.org.

Another rapidly evolving technology is telemedicine, which has vastly expanded, especially postpandemic. Telemedicine involves a video call between the patient and the psychiatrist or therapist. As most of our therapies do not need physical examination of the patients, telemedicine has been an ideal solution for psychiatric care. While some were skeptic of telemedicine being as effective as the office visit, research has shown equal benefits and a lot of flexibility. It saves patients time and resources as they won't have to worry about taking time off work, finding childcare, or needing transporta-tion to go to their visit. My personal experience is that patients are more

Figure 10.1 We use augmented reality technology for exposure therapy of phobias and PTSD. In this picture, you see my colleague Shantanu wearing the headset, which is connected to my computer via a wireless network. I see on my computer a three-dimensional map of his surrounding environment, where he is in that environment, and where he is looking at. I can then place dynamic feared objects (for example, a spider here) of different types, sizes, and colors, and define their behavior (for example, the spider crawling from the desk to the floor to the wall). Photo by author.

comfortably able to come to their virtual visits. I have even had police officers call me from their police cars during their lunchtime for their visits.

HOW TO SEEK HELP

It is sometimes difficult for people to navigate the healthcare system for their mental health needs. First question often is: Which professions do provide mental health services? The answer includes a relatively wide range of professionals. First line of care could be primary care doctors. If you are concerned that you are having too much anxiety and might need help, you can discuss it with your primary care doctor who can provide treatment herself, or refer you to a specialist. Most of the medications used for treatment of anxiety can be prescribed by an experienced primary care doctor.

Your doctor can also refer you to a therapist for psychotherapy. Both trained social workers and clinical psychologists can provide psychotherapy. You just need to check and see if they are trained in treating anxiety disorders, OCD, or PTSD. Some psychiatrists also offer psychotherapy, although many of them only prescribe medications. Psychiatrists, like myself, are medical doctors who have received at least four years of residency training in psychiatry to treat a wide range of mental illnesses including anxiety. Some, like myself, have more focused training in treatment of anxiety- and trauma-related conditions. Depending on the type of insurance you have, you may be able to directly reach out to a psychiatrist. If you are in psychotherapy, your therapist can refer you to a psychiatrist. Many clinics have both therapists and psychiatrists. Receiving care in such places will allows better coordination of care between your psychiatrist and therapist.

Some mental health providers do not accept insurance or only accept some insurance plans, which makes it difficult for a lot of people to receive care. You must see if the provider and their service are covered by your insurance. Alternatively, you can call your insurance and ask them for a list of mental health providers specialized in treatment of anxiety or PTSD (e.g., therapists who are trained in cognitive behavioral therapy) who are in their network and in your area.

Those who do not have insurance can reach out to a Community Mental Health (CMH) clinic or a Federally Qualified Health Center (FQHC) in their respective county.

Chapter 11

Riding the Beast

How to Use Fear to Our Advantage

You can discover what your enemy fears most by observing the means he uses to frighten you.

—Eric Hoffer, American philosopher

In our modern life, fear is often a disruptive force because its evolutionary purpose does not match the realities of our time. So far, most of this book has focused on why anxiety is so bothersome and troubling to our ability to enjoy and function optimally. But is it also possible to use this deeply ingrained mechanism to improve and boost our performance? Can fear be used in a positive way beyond its primitive function that is shaped for situations of physical threat? In this chapter I will explore the ways we can use fear to our advantage. My goal is not to explain how to overcome fear, but rather how to productively use it.

FEAR THAT WARNS US

The first step in dealing with fear is learning about what scares us. This is easily done in obvious situations of physical threat, but less so in modern-life anxieties. Fear is a sign that something is wrong, or "potentially" harmful. It is important to remember, our anxiety and fear are subjective estimates of what could be out there. Due to its crucial role in survival, fear has evolved to overestimate the risks; it is "better safe than sorry." The noise behind the bushes could be a predator, a murderer, or a bird or wind. But because the first two possibilities could kill us, they are prioritized in forming our reaction, despite their very low probability. We also learn to be afraid of things that are not really dangerous, or as dangerous as we think. Our previous experiences, culture and training, and imagination are part of this threat perception process.

In conclusion, fear "might" be a true warning sign, and always deserves attention, but with a critical mindset. As I have said before, fear is often a pin in the wrong chair that we are sitting on, a sign that we need to get off the chair. But first we have to see how big the pin is, or if the pin—or even the chair—is real!

When danger is determined to be real, the next step is determining the objective threat level. Even when a legit threat exists, based on their biology and past experiences, each individual might assess the threat level differently. While failing an exam does have consequences, extreme anxiety and panic attacks in the days prior to exam are not proportional to the level of potential risk. Too often we fail to have an objectively appropriate level of fear response, based on which we determine the level of danger. This means that we first get scared and then, based on this emotion, decide that what is out there must be bad. But being too scared does not always mean the risk is too high. Realistic risk assessment not only provides a better sense of control, but also allows dedication of appropriate mental, social, financial, and other resources to risk mitigation. Realistic risk assessment also allows us to achieve the optimal level of arousal needed for ideal performance.

OPTIMAL LEVEL OF AROUSAL

One function of fear is increasing the arousal level via sympathetic nervous system activation. Fear makes us more alert and awake, sharpens our attention, and increases our ability to focus on the task at hand. It also redirects our attentional resources to the problem to be solved, by prioritizing it over less relevant issues. The same mechanism is part of any situation where optimal performance is needed: a competition, an exam, an important artistic or physical performance or presentation, a determining meeting. In these situations, if we are too bored and our attention is scattered, we cannot perform ideally. We need some fire under us to get it together and focus.

But too much anxiety also disrupts attention, cognitive performance, and memory, and consequently the ability for optimal functioning. Ideal performance during stress needs an *optimal level of arousal*. We need to be anxious enough to be driven, be focused, and invest mental energy in the task at hand, but not too scared. If a student is bored and sleepy during an important exam, she will not do her best. She will also not have great memory if she is having a panic attack. If you wake up to a noise from downstairs in the middle of the night and are not even a bit scared, you will not be awake enough to respond fast if you face a burglar in the kitchen. But if you are terrified, the amygdala bypasses cognitive networks and you might reflectively punch your poor spouse who wanted to get some water. Studies have shown that both memory and attention require this optimal level of arousal for best outcomes.

In chapter 10 I described the treatment I have invented that uses augmented reality for exposure therapy of phobias and PTSD. When we used this technology for treating fear of spiders, all patients were able to touch a real live tarantula after less than one hour of treatment. I believe one of the reasons this treatment works so well, and beyond our initial expectations, is that it makes possible achieving the ideal level of arousal. The patient logically knows the AR spiders, snakes, dogs, or the crowd are not real, which helps them overcome their fear-based resistance to treatment. However, the animal brain that does distinguish real from unreal is terrified of these augmented digital objects. This automatic fear is reflected in both the patient's subjective response and their galvanic skin response. If patients did not experience any fear because they know the spiders are not real, treatment would not work. But too much fear at all levels of awareness would also interrupt the ability to engage in the treatment. The fear is just the right amount for the treatment to work.

The same principle applies in other psychotherapies, or for that matter, learning any new skills. Too low a level of arousal prevents enough motivation, attention, and persistence for learning, and too much fear impairs attention and memory, and causes procrastination.

By the way, a lot of our fears are as automatic, unusual, and unreal as the fear a patient experiences at the sight of the virtual spiders!

FEAR THAT MOTIVATES US

Fear can harness a great amount of mental and physical energy to be used in evading or neutralizing the threats we face. Fear stirs the needed motivation for action and change. The most primitive form of this motivation and energy is in the activation of the fight-or-flight sympathetic nervous system, resulting in increased heart rate, blood pressure, and physical preparedness. More complicated investment of this mental energy is in problem solving, planning, and taking strategic action. Too much fear, however, leads to freezing, or procrastination.

So, fear is the fuel that energizes our whole existence to take charge, act, and not delay. As I am writing this chapter, due to the brutal attack of Russia on Ukraine's civil infrastructures, most Ukrainian citizens have limited access to electricity right ahead of the winter. Many spend more than a day without electricity and running water. It is understandable for a nation to be afraid of one of the strongest (debatable now) armies in the world that has aimed at their subordination or annihilation. I admire how Ukrainians have channeled this fear energy into rapid, effective, and creative ways of fighting against the aggressor, and partnering with their allies. The purpose and meaning they have created for their fight for freedom have modified the fear to an optimal level. The collective energy of an optimal level of fear allowed this nation to unite, stand strong, and use all its resources to fend off the realistically appraised threat it is facing. In other words, they use fear, and don't let it use them.

The energy of fear and anxiety can be transformed into action in different ways. Fear not only enhances attention and motivation, but also can be used in avoiding procrastination and prioritizing tasks. Knowing that missing a deadline can have consequences can be used in prioritizing it over watching the movie that can wait for later. The other way we can use this energy is by learning skills and ways of dealing with the perceived threat. This happens in psychotherapy work: people need to be stressed enough to not only take action in seeking help, but also learn new coping skills, take on the internal conflicts, and participate in therapy. Preparation is another positive outcome of fear: in anticipation of meeting a close friend, we might just do some cleaning right before they arrive. When in-laws are visiting us for the first time, anticipatory anxiety motivates us to invest more energy in planning and making sure the space is pristine and towels and sheets are ready and available. If Ukrainians were not worried about the possibility of an invasion by their hostile and unpredictable neighbor, they would probably not be as prepared when the Russian army invaded their country. When the war started, if they had a wrong assessment of the threat, they would have been unprepared, or too terrified that they would give in. In these situations, fear of a danger can be used as a vaccine that immunizes us against that very threat.

In *The Lord of the Rings*, Gandalf is really dreading stepping inside the caves of Moria in anticipation of facing the fiery monster Balrog. But the monster in the water at the gate forces him and the fellowship to escape into Moria, and continue this necessary step of their journey. Sometimes fear is needed for overcoming procrastination. Fear of losing one's youth, productive age, and other opportunities to an unsatisfactory or abusive relationship motivates people to overcome the fear of being alone. By reminding ourselves of what we are losing or the negative consequences of the current situation, we can harness the fear it triggers, to make changes. I have previously mentioned that the prefrontal cortex, the cognitive brain and the nest of thoughts, can not only inhibit the amygdala's fear response, but also trigger fear in it. In this sense, we actually can stir fear in ourselves, and then use its energy to make change. We can use fear and anxiety to rile up the animal within, and cultivate its energy. We just need to be in command of the animal and lead it to the productive direction. This can also help distract it from unnecessary anxieties and destructive worries.

In chapter 14 I will talk about how political leaders stir fear in the masses all the time. But it is also true that an effective leader can use a realistic measure of fear in mobilizing a nation to make change, whether it is taking action to prevent climate catastrophes, or preparing to fend off an aggressor nation. In these situations, fear of losing resources, land, loved ones, and own lives motivates nations to channel this energy into actions, often heroic, to fend off the threats. The fear of what gun violence and mass shootings could do to their nation or their children can paralyze some, but might motivate others to take advocacy action and work for making society safer.

FEAR THAT MAKES US STRONGER

A reasonable level of fear and anxiety, when handled appropriately, can also strengthen our mental abilities and skills. This happens in different ways. One is by learning new skills to handle similar worrisome situations. We have all been there when certain occupational, academic, or social situations made us worried. Sometimes we kept avoiding them. But especially when they were not avoidable, we decided to take charge and learn how to resolve and handle the situation. During medical training, most doctors are nervous in new clinical situations they have not faced before. We often use that anxiety to read and learn more, watch videos, practice, and brainstorm with our colleagues, to be more prepared and comfortable in handling those clinical cases next time we face them. We can always try to learn better ways of coping with things that stress or scare us: more adaptive social skills, occupational techniques, ways of coping with our own conflicts, and resolving our own cognitive distortions and flaws that make us nervous in certain situations. Indeed, an important part of effective psychotherapy is using the motivation that is stirred by anxiety to learn more about oneself and acquire better coping skills. I always say anxious patients are the best; no one loves to be anxious. They come to my clinic already motivated for change, and I do not need to convince them that anxiety is not a good thing to have.

We can also use this energy for learning more about what we fear. I had a patient who loved surfing but was too afraid of sharks. We came up with a plan and he used that fear to learn more about sharks, their different types, those that were potentially dangerous, in which parts of the water near him they could dwell, how to avoid them, and so on. This knowledge helped him gain a more realistic sense of the perceived threat, and be able to swim while still relatively scared of sharks. Similarly, as fear is always a reaction within us to external or internal triggers, fear can be used to learn more about one-self, and the conflicts within.

FEAR THAT GROWS US

Every time we act despite our fear, we not only learn more about ourselves, the world outside, and how to handle challenges, but we also earn a reward-ing sense of control and agency. We begin to learn more about our abilities and strengths in facing the world outside. This part of our growth is portrayed in many folk stories and legends, such as when a young man, King Arthur, Aragorn, and many other heroes did not even imagine the strength they had, until they had their back to the wall and they had to pick up the sword. Many of us did not know what we had to offer and how strong we were, until we met the moment and had to endure the tough times and situations. Many heroes and great leaders rise to the occasion in tough situations, and become what they did not even know they were capable of becoming. Joan of Arc and the Ukrainian president Volodymyr Zelenskyy are examples. Most people did not imagine that Zelenskyy, a comedian turned president, would prove to be one of the bravest and toughest leaders in the face of immense aggression from a superpower. Many heroes themselves did not even imagine earlier what was in them that would come into fruition later. As we gain a stronger command of the world within by this growth, we also project a stronger image in the outside world, which positively impacts our relationships with others. The respect Zelenskyy has in the world now is incomparable with his international standing before the war started.

Fear and adversity can also make us wiser and put things in perspective. Those who have experienced real danger, have lost friends in war, and have been in the proximity of true threat to their existence, and were not broken, are often able to have a more realistic view of things. When you have feared for your life before, you might not worry as much about a disagreement at work or the possibility of losing a job or your favorite car. People who have survived adversities mature and become wiser in knowing what really mat-ters. Proximity to death is one of the purest moments of life that gives mean-ing to it. It is when things become real, and all the irrelevant and unimportant sides of the story vanish, and only reality remains. I have heard from soldiers how their losses and close encounters with danger in war have allowed them to see what really is scary, and what is not worth wasting fear.

USING EMPATHY AGAINST FEAR

Knowing fear and how it works within humans also allows handling aggression and threat coming from others. Bullies and thugs are often (whether by experience or by intuition) very familiar with fear and how it works in others. It is by the abuse of such knowledge that they succeed in gaining control over others and abusing them. But knowing fear and its working in us could also be used in a positive way. One who knows how fear works within one's mind and body could also use it to understand and fend off abuse of their vulnerabilities by others. When I know the vulnerabilities of my own psychology that a bully might try to take control of, I can more easily block them. I also know very well that the ones who abuse fear are very vulnerable to fear themselves! Finally, knowing fear and how it makes people vulnerable can help in an empathetic understanding of those who are scared, and their behavior. This understanding can even be used in helping them, as it has become my career.

> *The hero and the coward both feel the same thing, but the hero uses his fear, projects it onto his opponent, while the coward runs. It's the same thing, fear, but it's what you do with it that matters.*

> —Constantine "Cus" D'Amato, boxing trainer

Chapter 12

Fear and Meaning

Defining It before It Defines Us

There is nothing in the world, I venture to say, that would so effectively help one to survive even the worst conditions as the knowledge that there is a meaning in one's life.

—Viktor Frankl, Austrian psychiatrist and Holocaust survivor

As I mentioned at the beginning of this book, one of my favorite movies is *Life Is Beautiful*. This excellent work of Roberto Benigni tells the story of an Italian Jewish couple who are sent to a concentration camp during World War II. Unbeknown to the Nazis, the husband—Guido, starred by Benigni himself—brings his son Giosue to the camp and hides him. To protect his son from the horror of what is happening, Guido convinces Giosue that this is a game, and prisoners are players in this competition. Whoever plays by the rules and endures the cold, hunger, and other challenges will win the big tank that is parked in the camp yard. While everybody is terrorized by the ongoing atrocities and the thought of what lies ahead of them, Giosue is having fun in a concentration camp! Guido himself finds a meaning, a cause to fight, in helping to make sure his son will survive.

This movie does not intend to make light of the horrors of the Holocaust, but it is pointing at an important part of being human. We are creatures of meaning and narrative, and our feelings and emotions, both positive and negative, are affected by our unique and individual interpretation of our experiences. While dangerous and traumatic events in our environment can deeply affect us, the personal meaning each of us attribute to these experiences largely shapes the way we are touched by them. In other words, our perception of atrocities modulates the way they affect us.

Movies such as *Bad Times at the El Royale* or *Identity* show how multiple characters recall the same story, each from their own angle, perspective, and perception and misperception of what actually happened, what it meant, and as a result, arrive at a different conclusion. Each character not only has a different angle through which they view the events, but also brings their own past experiences, values, preconceptions, and ideals to the event. That is to say, they bring their own *subjectivity* to the picture, which colors their objective experience. This not only colors the experience, but also the perception of oneself and the others involved in it.

Serious real-life events, even when they seem equally experienced by those who go through them, still impact each individual differently. When a rocket explodes near a squad of soldiers in combat, in a simplistic approach (which sadly dominates our research of trauma), they all have the same experience, and sustain the same trauma. But in reality, there are a multitude of factors that can affect how each one of those soldiers experience the explosion. One soldier loses a close friend, and another does not. One soldier sees the torn dead body of his friend, has to deliver the message to his family, and lives the rest of his life with survivor's guilt and recurrent nighttime rumination on how he could have saved his friend's life. Another soldier gets injured. Another has his back to the explosion when it happens, then loses consciousness and does not see any of the gore scenes. One has previously lost friends to explosions, and reexperiences the horrific trauma. And the last member of the squad sustains a head injury that makes it difficult to process and recall the event properly. After the event, some might see themselves as lucky for surviving; others continue with survivor's guilt. For religious or spiritual soldiers, some grow doubts about their mission, some believe God saved them, others think this happened to them because God has abandoned them because they sinned. Others start questioning God's justice and fairness and keep contemplating on why this happened to them. These many different angles of perception, what each person brought with themselves to the experience, and the meaning they created after it happened, are just some of the aspects of how trauma impacts each person differently.

One of the pioneers in research of meaning in adversities is Viktor Frankl, an Austrian psychiatrist who himself was a Holocaust survivor. His renowned book *Man's Search for Meaning* is a story of his deep and painful experience and observations in the concentration camp. He made it his own purpose to learn what motivates people to keep fighting, and how people endure and survive the worst horrifying adversities. Frankl concluded that those who had, and maintained a sense of meaning and purpose, had a better chance of surviving in the concentration camp. He argued that a search for meaning is an integral and central function of the human mind, which keeps us hopeful and motivated in the face of adverse experiences. He turned his own excruciating experience of the Holocaust into an opportunity for helping others, self-observation, and trying to write his unfinished book in his mind (he did not have access to pencil and paper). A summary of his findings is this quote from his book: "What man actually needs is not a tensionless state but rather the striving and struggling for some goal worthy of him. What he needs is not the discharge of tension at any cost, but the call of a potential meaning waiting to be fulfilled by him." The foundation of *logotherapy*, a treatment developed by Frankl, is that finding a positive meaning in a negative experience deepens life, and mitigates the negative emotions.

Every day in the clinic, I see how the personal meaning of experiences affects the lives of my traumatized patients. Part of our mutual work with these patients is exploring and fine-tuning their interpretation of the trauma and their life after trauma to something more realistic and adaptive. I teach my students that people need a cause, a meaning, something to live for. If one wakes up, gets drive-through garbage food, sits all day at the desk they hate, gets drive-through garbage food on the way back home, and spends the night on the couch listening to angry cable news anchors, no medication can fill the gap of meaning in their life, or overcome the depression and anxiety caused by this lifestyle.

An important part of my research is trying to answer this fascinating question: How does personal meaning and interpretation of an experience affect the way we are touched or traumatized by that experience? Answering this question needs a book of its own, but I will share a summary of my research and clinical experience here.

WHAT SCIENCE TELLS US

To examine the biology of meaning in the laboratory, I began by exploring how different information given to people about the same aversive experience can affect the way their bodies react to it. Before receiving an injection, if someone is told "just a little pinprick," and another person is told that it will really hurt, their anticipatory anxiety about the same injection may be different. On the other hand, if the pain is overly underestimated, the unexpected nature of hurting might cause fear and mistrust.

In a fear conditioning and extinction learning experiment (see chapter 4 for a refresher), during the conditioning phase, participants learned that two stimuli (blue and yellow light) were associated with a loud noise. Prior to extinction learning, they were told that the yellow light would not be followed by the loud noise anymore, but no information was given about the blue light. During the extinction, none of the lights were followed by the noise. As expected, participants gradually began to learn that the blue light is safe now, as reflected in the gradual decline in their skin conductance response. For the yellow light, though, their bodily fear response quickly stopped. This means that the information about the yellow light not only was registered at a cognitive and conscious level, but also immediately impacted the automatic body response. Not surprisingly, in the fMRI scans, we found a larger activation in the prefrontal cortex when the participants viewed the yellow light. This finding is fascinating as it is one of the first research findings that shows that changing the higher-level cognitive meaning of a painful experience will have deep impact in the subconscious and automatic fear responses.

Then I began to research the personal meaning of experience of war and forced migration in refugees who were resettled in the state of Michigan. I have previously mentioned this longitudinal study of risk and resilience in refugees. We asked the refugees one simple question: "On a scale from 1 to 7, 7 being the worst thing that happened to you, how do you score your experience with the war and migration?" We also asked them to tell us how they felt about their physical health on a scale from "Excellent" to "Poor." We used detailed questionnaires to measure the level of their PTSD symptoms' severity.

What we found was very important: just that one question about how bad they ranked their experience of war and migration strongly predicted both the severity of their PTSD symptoms, and how healthy they felt. Those people whose scores of adversities were closer to 7 had a lot more PTSD symptoms, and felt less physically healthy.

This study provides some of the first research evidence that shows besides the painful experience itself, its perception is a very important factor in determining how our physical and mental health are impacted by it. In other words, there seems to be a connected way in which we perceive the outside world, and the world inside of our mind, and the body.

Cognitive reappraisal is the process of intentionally changing the cognitive narrative, meaning, or interpretation of a negative event. For example, when someone sees a snake, they can say to themselves, "This is a very dangerous snake," or change the narrative to, "This is a nonvenomous snake because I am in a place where venomous snakes rarely exist." A laboratory example is when the participants see a picture of a woman crying outside a church. They might first think that she is crying because she lost a loved one, and feel sad about it. Then they can change the narrative to, let's say, those are tears of joy because her best friend is getting married in the church.

Research shows that reappraising the negative experiences changes not only the emotions we experience, but also the way our brain processes them! In one cognitive reappraisal study, participants were asked to think of a less negative explanation for the angry or scared faces they saw on the screen. For example, they were asked to imagine that the angry-looking face belongs to someone who is getting pumped up and excited for a sporting event or is a model practicing expression of anger and is not really angry. Cognitive reappraisal lowered the negative emotion that the images caused, which was paired with an increased activation of the prefrontal cortex. This means that when we try to redefine a negative experience, the prefrontal cognitive brain gets engaged in modulating the negative emotions.

Other studies have found that a person's ability for reappraisal and creating a more positive meaning for their experiences not only increases their self-esteem, but also has a positive impact on their heart rate (possibly by reducing the sympathetic activity). Besides their current emotional response to what is happening now, cognitive reappraisal also impacts people's perspective on upcoming events by adjusting their attention and memories. When the person in the above snake example decides that the snake is, say, a pet snake, he will then get a chance of noticing the beautiful colors of the snake, its smooth moves, or the nice-looking tank it is housed in. The individual who decided the woman outside the church is crying tears of joy might then remember good memories of her own wedding when a very close friend was joyfully tearful.

The research studies I just reviewed show from an experimental science standpoint the wisdom that has been expressed by many thinkers throughout history.

> *If you are distressed by anything external, the pain is not due to the thing itself, but to your estimate of it; and this you have the power to revoke at any moment.*

—Marcus Aurelius

THE TWO-WAY ROAD BETWEEN MEANING AND ADVERSITY

The cognitive lens through which we see the world affects how we perceive adverse events. A religious person has a specific global cognitive system within which events and experiences are understood and interpreted and emotional reactions are built upon. Someone who sees life experiences as success or failure, when facing a scary or traumatic experience, has to fit it within the context of winning or defeat. For this person, fear of loss is often bigger than the trauma itself. On the other hand, a situation not too scary to others, for example, losing the chance of a career promotion, might be terrifying for this person. Culture, religion, past experiences, what is learned from the family, and what others expect of us—these all can impact the meaning we create for a given experience.

On the other hand, tough experiences also change our global perspective. As a highly adaptive species, we continue to learn from our experiences and adjust our perspective, values, and preconceptions. This tendency allows us to fine-tune our approach to a constantly changing world and adapt and cope with new challenges and opportunities. But highly traumatic experiences can disproportionally affect our perception of the world and our meaning system. That is because anything related to survival has a top priority in our emotional and learning system, and is coded deeper than other knowledge.

Trauma challenges our beliefs about safety, fairness, humanity, kindness, and how the universe works. Extreme or repeated trauma, especially, deeply tests our meaning system by violating the assumptions we had about ourselves, others, and the world. Those who are able to make sense of and integrate painful experiences into their global meaning system may be more successful in dealing with the emotional pain. But sometimes trauma and adversity shatters one's preexisting understanding of the world and how it works. I have seen too often how rape, assault, or shootings make people lose their trust in others, doubt their religious beliefs, or lose their sense of control and agency.

Trauma at the collective and group level can change meanings and approaches to life, social and personal perspectives, and cultures for generations of people and nations. In a collective trauma like the Holocaust, pain and horror not only affects those who lived it (whether via personal exposure, or by feeling the threat from a distance), but also the generations to follow. This intergenerational transmission of trauma not only happens at an epigenetic level as I explained in chapter 9, but also by changing collective perception of the existential threat, and transmission of threat-related behaviors, perspectives, and traditions. Catastrophes perpetrated by humans affect not only the victims of the atrocious actions, but also those who are in some way linked with the aggressors. For example, Germans during World War II, or Russians during and after the war on Ukraine, had and will have to deal with the new national identity, shame and guilt whether they were for or against those actions, and a deep confusion about who they are now as a nation.

LESSONS I HAVE LEARNED IN THE CLINIC

As a trauma expert practicing in urban Detroit metro, I regularly work with people who are trying to make sense of their painful experiences. An integral and important part of my treatment work is helping people answer fundamental questions that are raised by their traumatic and stressful experiences, and evaluate and fine-tune the way they have interpreted them. Regardless of my own perspective on life, my role is to help my patients incorporate their experiences in their own world of meanings and values. For this to happen, I need to understand their historical background, culture, religion, philosophy of life, fears, hopes, and visions. Then I assess how trauma has challenged or changed their worldview, and how they have defined the experience in relation to themselves and the world around them. The next step is to see how realistic and adaptive this interpretation is, and if it is helping them to cope or causing distress and dysfunction.

I recall that in one of my visits with a young anxious patient, Tiffany, whose anxiety was well controlled before, she seemed very worried and depressed. I learned that it was because she had come out as homosexual and was in a loving relationship with another woman. Coming from a strict religious background, Tiffany was terrified of her family's reaction if they learned about. it. "My grandmother thinks I will go to hell!" she said.

I am more on the spiritual side than religious. But I have gained a fine understanding of the major religions. In my own search for meaning, I was always curious to learn about major religions and philosophies humans have adopted to define their own existence and the world surrounding them. I could easily imagine how terrifying it could be for a religious person to think they have to choose between leaving their partner and going to hell. "What would Jesus say?" I asked. Without much thinking she immediately answered, "He wouldn't care!," to which I replied, "I would go with what Jesus says over what my grandmother says." Tiffany smiled and looked relieved. Without me changing her medications, Tiffany's anxiety declined to its mild baseline level. By this example, I am not suggesting that changing meaning and resolving conflict is always easy and quick. At times it takes a lot more work to get there.

Survivors of torture, assault, rape, and other atrocities perpetrated by humans often ruminate about why this happened to them. That is because our brains have a causational approach and always look for a cause for the events. That mechanism is meant to help us predict and prevent future similar events. Based on a multitude of factors, different people may speculate different causes for their trauma. Some feel guilty and think they must have done something wrong to deserve a punishment. Some begin to believe the world is a hostile environment and that others cannot be trusted. Others believe that the trauma has changed them and now they are incomplete, damaged, or less of a human. I have seen survivors of rape or abuse who thought they were chosen by the predator because they dressed or acted in a specific way, a belief that is sometimes enforced by society. Having an objective understanding becomes more challenging in abusive relationships where the abuser is skilled in instilling the idea that the victim did something wrong to deserve the abuse.

In many cases, I work against people's desire for creating a meaning or reason for why things happen. I help my patients understand the abuse, assault, rape, or war had nothing to do with who they are and what they did. They are not responsible for what someone else did to them. They just happened to be in the wrong place at the wrong time. They happened to live in the region that was struck by war, were walking in the alley where a robber or a sexual predator was looking for prey, or happened to trust the wrong person. In other words, often there is no self-referential meaning where we are searching for a meaning! Overinterpretating or overrelating events to what we did, or who we are, will unnecessarily complicate our emotions.

Guilt (including survivor's guilt) and shame are common emotions of survivors of trauma and those who have witnessed suffering in others. I see this guilt a lot in first responders. Their job dictates a sense of control and the ability to rescue others. It is also the nature of their job that they often fail to save a life despite their best efforts. When a child dies after an unsuccessful CPR, they lose a partner in a shooting, or cannot pull people out of a burning car soon enough, some first responders end up ruminating for days, months, or even years about what they could have done differently, or what they might have done wrong. I have seen them plagued by sleepless nights, nightmares, and daily flashbacks of the event, and the guilt that sucks out the joy of their lives. I have to keep reminding them that hindsight is 20/20, and that at the moment of the incident they did the best they could do. Their peers tell them the same thing.

Chronic exposure to negative life experiences and trauma in people like first responders and survivors of abuse, human trafficking, and war sometimes leads to skewing their worldview. They begin to believe that the world is a dangerous place, life is brutal and heartless, and people cannot be trusted. Their unique experiences color and alter their view of themselves, the world, and humanity, as they have repeatedly seen the worst of what humans do to each other. It is as if I were to decide that most humans are anxious or depressed because I see too many anxious and depressed people in my clinic. I sometimes even have to remind myself that I have an unusual exposure to stories of the worst human experiences and things humans do to each other, and this should not affect my general perspective on humanity.

Traumatic and hard experiences do not always create negative meanings. As in the case of Viktor Frankl, positive and deep perspectives risen out of pain could change people for the better and deepen their worldview, or offer an opportunity for humane acts of sacrifice and altruism. We see and hear this so often in times of war when heroism of some becomes exemplary. Trauma can also strengthen people's character, and help them develop a deeper meaning for life and its experiences. The documentary *The Elephants and the Grass*, by the brilliant director (and my good friend) Brandon Gulish, which I have noted in chapter 7, is the story of a Sudanese refugee mother and daughter. Having gone through the worst horrors of war and torture themselves, Shamira and her mother turn their pain into action in helping and protecting others. In the US, there are those who have turned their frustration and pain of losing a loved one to a mass shooting to activism to make their society safer. People are sometimes not even aware of their resilience and heroism. I frequently remind my first responders that there are few who would be willing to put their own life on the line to do what they do: protect and save others. Although they have not been able to save some, their work has positively impacted the life and livelihood of many. I remind a refugee parent the beauty of their sacrifice and resilience that has brought their children to safety for a better future, and a survivor of human trafficking the strength they had to survive and strive against the horrible atrocities they had to experience.

As a trauma psychiatrist, I also have to deal with my own vicarious exposure to trauma. I see too many people who have survived torture, abuse, war, and human trafficking, or have witnessed the worst of what humans do to each other. Listening to their stories is often painful and sometimes leaves me nauseous for days. At times I ask myself, "How much longer can I do this?" What helps me in those tough moments is remembering my purpose: helping others get better, and knowing that the man devastated by trauma who is sitting in front of me, in a few weeks or months will be feeling much better. That is the meaning that I as a physician have created for my own exposure to suffering and pain.

Chapter 13

Fear and Creativity

Monsters that We Forge, and Monsters that Forge Us

>*I still do get terribly nervous, and that's partly due to the fact I think too much and overanalyze things. I'll start worrying about my parents or my dog, and I'll picture him opening the window of my apartment and falling out, even though I can't get that thing open myself.*

—Amanda Seyfried, American actress

While fear and creativity might seem opposing on the surface, they are overlapping mental forces. Fear is focused on our most basic need for survival. On the contrary, creativity is free to work best when our basic survival needs are met. Besides, while fear is a very primitive function that we share with less evolved animals, creative arts, science, and culture are the most evolved and abstract aspects of humanity that profoundly distinguish us from other animals. On the other hand, fear and creativity both are to a large extent automatic, unconscious, and intuitive. While cognitive processing is always a part of it, the greatest works of creativity are not just the result of conscious logical thinking. Artists, writers, and scientists spend weeks and months waiting for it "to happen," and often themselves cannot clearly explain how it works in their mind. In other words, there is no clear algorithm that can be used for creating great products. I often compare it to pregnancy. The art grows inside the artist autonomously while the artist keeps feeding it, and when the time comes, delivery happens. In that sense, there is a lack of full conscious control over both fear and creativity, and their work in our minds.

But how do fear and creativity affect and color each other? We know that fear is deeply ingrained in us at a personal and societal level, and that anxiety disorders are very common. That means many artists, writers, and scientists have dealt with fear and anxiety in themselves, some we know about, and some we do not. What happens to creative people struggling with anxiety, and how can a creative mind overcome, or drown in anxiety? How could the existential terrors of wars or oppression of their time have affected the work of artists and scientists?

HOW FEAR IMPACTS CREATIVITY

I have previously explained the close connection between our emotions, memories, attention, and cognitive function. Emotions can prioritize recall of certain memories, shift our attention to what they find most relevant in our environment, and affect what we think about. As a top priority emotion, fear basically colors all of our basic and advanced mental processes. When we are scared, our attention is directed to signs of threat and away from neutral or pleasant stimuli. Fear- and danger-related memories needed for self-protection are easier to recall, and too much fear impairs memory. When we're scared, our thinking is invested in worrying about what could go wrong. Since creativity needs to use all the above mental function for its work, it will be impacted by fear and anxiety.

The simplest way fear and anxiety affect creativity is by impairing and distorting attention, concentration, memory, energy, and sense of agency. On the other hand, optimal creative performance requires peak concentration, a high level of mental energy, and investment of thinking and memory in a highly complicated mental (and often physical) task. Anxiety also sees creative work as a lower priority mental functioning, as opposed to measures that are needed to reduce or neutralize the perceived threat. For example, if I am too worried about a class that I will be teaching tomorrow, I will not be in the mood, be able to focus, or have the mental energy that I need to seriously focus on writing this book. My mind will be busy worrying about the class, thinking about what could go wrong tomorrow, and reviewing my slides over and over to make sure I will not make a mistake. So, despite the common romanticism in pop culture, mental illness, including anxiety disorders, are not good for creativity. Just the fact that some brilliant artists suffered from a mental illness does not mean that mental illness promotes creative work. I would argue that an artist without an anxiety disorder would do better than with it.

Fear also regresses us to a more primitive, rigid, and less flexible level; and rigidity is generally the opposite of creativity. It is safer to go down the known and more predictable path when scared. To be safe than sorry, when scared, we stick with what has proven or is accepted to work rather than try-ing to find new ways. If terrified of death, most people retreat to the older and more established cultural and religious beliefs about their immortality, instead of trying to explore other explanations about what happens when someone dies. But for some people who do not find the available explanations about afterlife soothing, the opposite can happen. For example, because creative work usually lasts much longer than the creator, fear of death may encourage creative work that gives the creator a sense of immortality through their creation. They will symbolically continue to live in their work, and in the eyes and minds of those who come after them and see, read, or use their work. I myself know that after I am gone, some of my scientific discoveries, teachings, treatments, ideas, and writings will continue to live through others. In fact, you might be reading this book long after I am gone!

So far I have explained how internal anxiety affects innovation and creativity. But fear has also very often limited, or even killed, creativity from outside. The group—in both of its concrete (the tribe) and abstract (colleagues in the same field of science) forms—often resists highly different ideas and ways of life that are perceived as abnormal or unusual, or against the established culture, philosophy, religion, or even science. From an evolutionary perspective, this is an effort by the tribe and its leaders to keep the group in harmony and united around the same ways of thinking and living. History is filled with examples of how the group often has ignored, denied, mocked, or even oppressed the unusual and innovative thinking. People with different views on roles, rights, cultural norms (e.g., women's and minorities' rights), modern scientific ideas (doubting that earth is the center of the universe, or suggesting common biological roots with other animals), or art that has been "too" innovative have often faced strong resistance and denial. True innovation usually needs a level of independent thinking to overcome the fear of marginalization by the tribe.

Beyond the usual group resistance, oppression by the less democratic governing forces, or occupiers, have played a significant role in confining creative work. Ideologies, whether the medieval Catholic Church, Communism, or the Taliban, have been and are comfortably brutal in silencing thinkers, artists, journalists, and scientists who have decided to think differently. A very common theme in dystopian fiction is forcing everyone to look and think alike, and seeing different as dangerous. While creative thinking is an engine for growth in democratic societies, oppressive regimes do not like it, unless it is in the service of promoting their ideologies and political gains.

As fear can take over all our mental energy, it can also be a great motivator of creativity, but in its own service. Fear and anxiety color creativity both at personal and collective levels, to show the worries, to find new ways of feeling less worried, or to fend off the perceived threat more effectively. This happens at both concrete and abstract levels. For example, American anthropologist Ernest Becker argues that to avoid the anxiety of their mortality, humans create cultural beliefs and complicated stories that portray them as immortal. In his theory, existential fear of death has throughout history employed the collective creativity of humans to find or forge a calming solution for this terror. The complicated myth, artwork, and elegant architecture and crafts the Egyptians have created to overcome this fear of annihilation after death, and maintain a sense of immortality, is a fascinating example.

Investing enormous amounts of scientific and technological research in developing military defense systems and weaponry has always been an integral part of any society. In fact, military research has always been on the cutting edge of science, and many of the technologies we use, like the internet, are the product of military research. This is in part due to the instinctive ambitions of dominating others and their resources, but more importantly, out of fear of destruction by others.

As I have explained previously, for optimal performance, we need to have some level of anxiety within the optimal window of arousal. Being bored slows and demotivates us, and being terrified freezes us. If too terrified, the person or the nation might freeze, or retreat to the most basic functions and most familiar ways of self-preservation. Realistic fear and anxiety, on the other hand, utilizes creativity and innovation to increase the chance of survival at the personal and group level. There is also a dark side to this. In the next chapter, I will explain the ways creativity is abused in the service of unrealistic and illusionary fears, or enslaved to the ambitions of the tribe leaders.

In summary, like any other emotion, fear can stir creativity in its own direction. The same way the universal emotion of love has abundantly colored our songs, paintings, myths, and even science, as another deeply ingrained emotion, fear has done the same. Our art and literature have always been filled with fear, anxiety, and terror, whether in the form of Munch's painting *Scream*, or folk stories of witches and demons, or zombie movies. Submitting to our worst fears, or ambitions of terrorizing others, our scientific creativity has been used for inventing demons like nuclear weapons.

HOW CREATIVITY AFFECTS FEAR AND ANXIETY

A creative mind can both cause or limit fear. Because it requires a willingness to venture outside of the comfort zone and into the unknown, creativity can often stir fear. To create, one must break ties with the status quo and standard and established norms. This usually leads to predicted and unpredicted challenges, opposition by the group, and fear of failing to create something both good and accepted by others. All of these constraints can scare the creator and slow them from actively pursuing their creative goals. The cultural and tribal opposition to creative work that denies the established norms is not limited to embarrassment of failure or humiliation. It also involves loss of important resources. Innovative and creative ideas have historically cost prominent artists and scientists dearly—in the case of Galileo, almost his life! The more novel an idea, the harder it is for the average tribe members to distinguish it from scam or heresy (in religious, artistic, or scientific ways of it). Now-famous artists like Monet and Van Gogh were not accepted well during their time. Dr. Ignaz Semmelweis, who suggested surgeons should wash their hands before operating on a patient, was for years ridiculed by his peers. In academia, junior researchers are often warned against stepping outside the shadow of their mentors and established scientists, as their innovative ideas are evaluated as risky or absurd. Besides that, any new direction in science needs a lot of new work and complicated planning in uncharted territories, which understandably increases the risk of failure compared to the "known" path. Often the innovators themselves are not even sure if their ideas are brilliant or stupid!

So depending on the degree of novelty and needed work, there is always a level of stress, risk, unknown, problem solving, and potential social resistance met by highly creative work. The balance between these risks and fears, the perceived reward, creator's previous experience (success of failure in creative adventures), and their biology (trait anxiety, openness to novelty, and dependence on external reward) determine how willing someone is to explore the unknown, and how scared they will be facing it.

Challenges that life throws at us often require adaptation, creative thinking, and action. In that sense, creativity could not only save lives or assets, but also help reduce stress and anxiety by solving the challenges one is facing. Historically, wartime and recessions have boosted creative production and scientific growth and development. This is because such conditions demand finding different ways than what we already had before we faced the challenge. Those who were not able to be creative and adapt lost to nature or other tribes. In this sense, creativity is not only triggered by stress, but also reduces stress by resolving its source and providing us with a better sense of control over our challenges. When we know we can do something about it, it is less scary than when we are helpless and hopeless in the face of adversity.

Creativity can also give us more adaptive meaning and interpretation for adverse experiences. During wartime, art, philosophy and literature have offered positive national identity and motivation. The painted picture of Rosie the Riveter is one piece of art with a lasting strong cultural meaning and impact. Creative minds also directly target anxiety and fear by finding better coping skills and ways of solving problems. Some of us are using our creative abilities for understanding fear and anxiety, and innovative ways of treating it. Many of those in this line of work are at least in part motivated by their own struggles with anxiety, or that of their loved ones.

A creative mind can also transform and sublimate its fears and anxieties into art, science, literature, and other products. Artists can externalize their fears and anxieties to mitigate their internal psychic impact. What scares them is changed and transformed, projected onto something outside and distant, or displaced with something more tolerable.

Conversely, the same way a creative mind can find better solutions, it can also create more complicated problems and imagine more things to worry about. Actually, writing this chapter was motivated by a discussion I had about a creative patient with one of my colleagues. We were both amazed by how his mind was able to find and create complicated catastrophic scenarios that could happen in his life. His creative mind always went on to invent a new problem for each solution that was offered for his worries. Like Stephen King can create the most sophisticated horror stories and scenarios from which escape is almost impossible, a creative anxious mind can think of very inventive and complicated ways things in their life could go wrong. In this case, creativity marries anxiety; it becomes fear's ally in scaring the creative minds, and those around them.

Chapter 14

Fear that Rules Us

Politics of Fear

When Mexico sends its people, they're not sending their best. . . . They're sending people that have lots of problems, and they're bringing those problems with us. They're bringing drugs. They're bringing crime. They're rapists.

—Donald J. Trump, June 16, 2015

Disclaimer: I am not a political expert, neither do I have strong political affiliations. In this chapter and across the book, I have tried to keep my own political views out of the discussion and follow a scientific approach. Many of the examples that I use in this chapter are about Trump only because of the historical concurrence and bold clarity of those examples.

In chapter 4 I explained how evolution has equipped us with different ways of learning what is potentially dangerous to us, our tribe, and our assets. Besides personal experience, an advantageous and efficient way of learning about threats is by social signaling. This can happen via observation of another human's encounter with danger, or verbal or written information relayed to us by other humans. This has served us tremendously, as not all of us have to face the same danger to learn to avoid it next time. If a tribe member noticed a predator in a part of territory, the rest of us would avoid that area. If one member saw another tribe's army approaching, all of us would prepare quickly to defend our territory. We still use this capability.

The more dangerous the threat and the higher the likelihood of harm, the more we trust the messengers. You may hate, mistrust, and dislike a neighbor. But if they told you there is an armed robber on the loose in the neighborhood, you would probably get inside and lock all the doors—better safe than sorry. You might even brainstorm with that neighbor about how to protect

139

your families in case the shooter showed up near your houses. From an evolutionary standpoint, this increased within-group trust and unity in times of danger is an advantage that increases our likelihood of survival. When facing serious threat, people often set aside their less important disagreements and come together to fend off the common danger more effectively. That is why in times of war nations are more united and at least for a short time set aside many of their disagreements and differences.

We have also learned that fear is not meant to follow logic, and that it is rather fast than accurate. In the context fear has evolved, it is more important to immediately escape, or neutralize a threat, than think analytically about its nature and deeper intentions. The problem, though, is that the primitive threats our fear circuitry has evolved to fend off were very different than the complicated situations of modern life and societies of our age. While we were set to immediately attack or run away when we noticed a predator, today's life threats are better dealt with through logical thinking. The illogical and impulsive nature of fear is an important element in the politics of fear.

WE ARE A TRIBAL SPECIES

Like other primates, we are a very tribal and group-oriented species. This is not necessarily bad; it is actually a key to our survival. Our species has made tremendous progress in culture, civilization, science, literature, and technology, because of our ability to connect, work and hunt together, protect each other, and unite against calamities the harsh nature has thrown at us. We are more successful and safer as a group. However, due to our tribal nature, arguably the most dangerous threat to us has always been other humans. Wars and destruction between tribes, ideologies, and nations have always been part of being human. We have always fought and killed each other out of fear of loss or wish of expansion.

This tribalism and group-oriented nature, combined with a sense of competition, is present in many aspects of our modern life: we have countries, religious affiliations, group sports, and creative competitions, and we are usually very serious about these affiliations. Competitive sports are among the biggest industries, and sports fans rarely leave their teams. We are even less logical about them: fans of both teams pray for their team to win, as if God would take sides in a football match. Fans stay loyal to a team for a lifetime regardless of how bad that team is. Similarly, people rarely leave behind their religious, political, or national affiliations.

WHAT SCIENCE SAYS ABOUT OUR TRIBAL NATURE

Social neuroscience is a fascinating field of research that aims at understanding the human brain in the context of social and cultural interactions. This type of research has shed light on how differently our brains perceive people who look and think like us, compared to those who do not. For example, we know that we react more strongly to emotions—especially agony—of members of the group we relate to, compared to the outgroups. In an study of brain responses in native Japanese people in Japan and Caucasians in the US, researchers found that each group had a larger amygdala response to fearful faces of members of their own cultural group. This can be seen as an evolutionary advantage, as a threat to someone who looks more familiar may be more likely to threaten us also. Whatever is scaring one of our group members, it is potentially dangerous to us also. Interestingly, these differences become less prominent in bicultural people, like Japanese Americans, and those growing up around people of different backgrounds since earlier ages. This is a very important finding that means our perception of who is one of "us" and who is not is not necessarily hardwired—it is learned. What is hardwired is an affinity to group affiliation.

Group-oriented empathy is even visible in more abstract affiliations developed later in life. In an interesting study, Australian researchers looked at how college students perceived harm to their collegemates compared to students of a competing university. University of Queensland students were shown videos of someone intentionally hurting another person (e.g., beating them with a broomstick). In different video clips the actors were identified as members of the University of Queensland, or the competing university, Queensland University of Technology. Participants were more sensitive when they saw that someone from their university was being beaten. Researchers also found an increased activation in a part of the prefrontal cortex linked with moral judgment, the orbitofrontal cortex.

Although these studies show differences in how our brains perceive and process social cues, emotions, and threats in "us" vs. "others," they do not necessarily mean that we are "hardwired" for it. Rather, they suggest an inherent tendency for group affiliation, which can be learned. I want to emphasize this point as it negates the idea that racism or any other prejudice is an inherent and biological part of being human. We are trained and educated to conceive a group as ours, and another as others. This capacity, however, is a biological loophole that has been abused by tribe leaders throughout history.

THE POLITICS OF FEAR

Our strong tendency for group affiliation and trusting our tribe members when facing danger, the illogical nature of fear, and its tendency for aggression have always been used by tribe leaders, ideologies, and religions to subordinate the tribe and dominate the others. Those seeking power have quickly learned that when scared, we are susceptible to regressing to more primitive and automatic reactions of the human animal. Fear of "the others" has always been used to turn millions of humans to illogical cold weapons, acting like an army of ants. Reviewing our history as a species, it is astonishing to see how many times millions have accepted terribly flawed ideologies and have blindly followed their leaders to unimaginable destruction of others and themselves.

THE POLITICS OF FEAR COOKBOOK

In 2016, a CNN crew came to Detroit to film a report on my research on war trauma and stress of migration in Syrian and Iraqi refugee families. After interviewing me, they went to the community to talk to refugee families. When the interview was aired, I asked my students who saw it, "What do you think was the most impactful part of this interview?" Each student guessed about the most important research data I had shared with the reporters. I, however, had a different opinion: it was none of what I had said. I believe the most important part of that report was a Muslim mother walking on the street with her cute and innocent children. Those few seconds put a human face on what to many people was just a concept. I said to my students, "It should be hard to see these innocent, cute children and still hate them!"

For leaders to take advantage of our biological and psychological tendency for tribalism, they first need to define an "us" that is distinct from others. The "us" has often been people of one nation, even though borders of nations have largely changed throughout history. For the citizens of the Persian Empire two thousand years ago (that covered most of current Iran, Iraq, Turkey, Afghanistan, Pakistan, and other countries), "us" included a much larger number of people, races, religions, and ethnic groups than it does in Iran of today. While look, land, and religion are easier ways of defining the "us," for the abstract beings like humans, the number of ways a group can be defined is countless. What matters most is a categorically defined and distinct characteristic that is shared by the target people. A tribe can have a fluid nature and be defined differently at different times. During World War II, being a Nazi defined a distinct tribe within the German nation. But now, Germany is part of the North Atlantic Treaty Organization (NATO), committed to defending the countries it was in war with decades ago. In the United States, what defines a Republican or a Democrat and the geographical distribution of these two tribes have substantially changed since they were established. Even within one tribe, depending on the leaders' ambitions at a moment, different aspects of the tribal identity such as land, religion, political affiliation, or race may be highlighted at different times. In the United States, politics sometimes focus on patriotism, sometimes on Christianity, and sometimes on capitalism.

The next step is defining a "them," a group that has one or a few clear and distinct differences with us. Like what defines "us," these differences could be more tangible like race, land, and religion, or more abstract. What facilitates digesting the "them" vs. "us" dichotomy is humans' tendency for a binary approach to things, especially with emotions like fear. When scared, something is either safe or dangerous; there is no middle ground. Depending on the leaders' interest, "us" and "them" could be Middle Eastern people, Sikhs, Jews, liberals, conservatives, White people, Black people, Christians, the Left, the Right, or any label that draws a line between the two target groups. The abstract borders can easily be redefined, and those tribe members who disagree with the plan could be expelled from the tribe. We saw this many times during Trump's presidency when he redefined any Republican politician who disagreed with him as a RINO, or Republican in name only.

Next step: "They" are bad. To spice up the "us" vs. "them" dynamics with fear and hate, "they" must be presented as a threat to us. They are portrayed as wanting to either hurt us, or take our limited resources and dilutable precious "things." Depending on what leaders want to achieve, the things can be our land, food, life, assets, culture, race, guns, jobs, or freedom. Sometimes they don't even want to take our things, they just hate them and want to destroy them. On March 9, 2016, Trump said in an interview, "I think Islam hates us." He basically decided to turn nearly a third of the world's population into a dangerous concept. The "us" was Americans, and the "them" was Islam. It did not even matter that this sentence did not even make sense. Islam as a religion was born more than a thousand years before the United States existed, and it is impossible for that Islam to have hated America. Even if by Islam he meant to refer to Muslims of the current time, it would be practically impossible to put 1.8 billion Muslims of different cultures, races, nationalities, and political beliefs from all over the world, including in the US itself, in one category. At the time it was said, that sentence was meant to relay a message to the target audience that there is a thing called Islam, whose people hate our existence and should not be allowed in this country. But this concept was very soon redefined. It did not take long before Trump was having a great time dancing with Saudi leaders in Saudi Arabia, one of the most extreme Islamic governments in the world. Even when *Washington*

Post reporter Jamal Khashoggi was brutally murdered by the Saudis in 2018, Trump's response was redefining them as business partners who were buying billions of dollars of military equipment from us.

While tribalism is often used against other nations, over the recent years it has more and more penetrated internal US politics. Trump was never shy about classifying many Americans as enemies. Repeatedly he claimed that Democrats wanted to destroy the United States. He did not suggest that their policies were wrong or that they were misguided. No, he told his supporters many times that they intentionally aimed at destroying the country they represent. He also claimed that those traitors stole the election in 2020. To someone who had wholeheartedly accepted Trump as the leader of this nation who has access to correct information, the next logical step was to believe what the leader says. If there is a group of Americans (here Democrats) who hate this country, and stole its democracy, hating them would be the next logical step. I in no way want to justify the criminal acts of the January 6, 2021, insurrection of the US Capitol. They were wrong, dangerous, and at best extremely misguided. But I could imagine some of those people were just following their leader. In their mind, their democracy was stolen, and they saw themselves as saviors and soldiers of that very democracy.

"They" Are Less Than "Us"

Popular movies and TV shows like *Alien*, *Terminator*, *Independence Day*, and *The Walking Dead* all share a main theme. The human race is endangered by an extremely lethal "them" that want to destroy us all. There is an aspect of "them" in such movies filled with violence, that makes it easy for the viewers to watch, and even enjoy with delight, killing and destruction of "them." But how can we enjoy death and destruction of others? Most people felt hurt when a dog was killed in the movie *John Wick*, so why was it so easy to enjoy (or be neutral) to his brutal killing of hundreds of humans in the same movie?

The distinction is that besides the fact that "they" hate us, we fear them, and defending ourselves is justified; they are less human than us. They are machines, nonhuman aliens, or humans who have already died (zombies), or are morally below us. In movies where the "heroes" and the audience enjoy killing the "bad guys," you never see the villains having a loving dinner with their family or playing with their kids. They are pure evil who only sadistically enjoy tormenting innocent people. This kind of portrayal also happens in the real world. The enemy is shown as uncivilized, heartless, evil, and less human, a far concept that is *very* different than "us."

Nazis portrayed Jews as lesser humans. Many Russians were happy to see the Russian army brutally killing Ukrainians because their government had convinced them that those Ukrainians were "Nazis." During the Islamophobic period of Hollywood, Muslims were portrayed as uncivilized, extremely mean, and heartless people, who were always violently screaming and shouting something in Arabic. You would never see a Muslim man play with his child in the park or fall in love. In modern politics, Trump used this strategy to belittle his opponents by attacking their character or physique. He called Michael Bloomberg "Mini Mike" because he was shorter, Jerry Nadler "fat Jerry," Nancy Pelosi "crazy Nancy," Marco Rubio "little Marco," and the list goes on.

For "us" to believe what we are told about "them," leaders try their best to keep "them" and "us" separated. That is because it is easier to accept what we are told about people, when we have never interacted with them to learn who they are by our own experience. Furthermore, when scared, we are less likely to want to reach out and connect. It is easier to fear, hate, and destroy what we do not know. If you grew up only around people who looked like you, only listened to one media outlet, and only heard from your old uncle about those who look or think differently, you would be more likely to accept what you are told about "them."

Once a soldier told me, "It is much easier to kill someone you have never met, from a distance. When you look through the scope, you just see a red dot, not a human." The less we know about the others as humans, the more disconnected we are, and the easier it is for us to hate and destroy them. They become a concept we have never met.

TRIBALISM, FEAR, AND AGGRESSION

A recent phenomenon in US politics, which has been worsening every day, is the intolerance of the "different." Many have stopped to welcome different views and perspectives, and anything different is portrayed as dangerous by the leaders and their affiliated media. When the different is seen as a threat, it needs to be neutralized; it needs to be destroyed. Different should not be listened to, because you do not listen to your enemy. I have previously explained how aggression is very often a reaction to fear. In the face of a perceived threat, we either avoid and escape it, or attempt to neutralize and destroy it. Throughout our history, fear has been used to turn humans to the most mindless ruthless weapons willing to destroy nations and millions of people defined under a feared label. When we are fed with a threat of destruction by "them" who hate us and are less than us, we choose to not be the destroyed, but the destroyer. When scared and angry, we are less logical, more trusting of our leaders, and more united under the banner of tribe that is defined for us. The mobilized human animal then is willing and able to perpetrate barbarities unimaginable to the civilized human. For example, to most people in their right mind, it is unbelievable that more than fifty million civilians died in World War II, just less than a century ago.

Although aggression is most palpable in its concrete form of war and killing of others and destruction of their resources, it could have more abstract presentations. Destruction of their properties and their religious or cultural landmarks, forcing them to leave their lands, and harassing them are other forms of aggression. In the day and age of digital tribalism, harassing them on social media or blocking and removing them from our awareness are other symbolic ways of aggression.

IS THERE A SOLUTION?

"Reach Out to Trump Supporters," They Said. I Tried. I give up.—New York Times opinion piece by Wajahat Ali, November 19, 2020

There is little doubt that in recent years US politics has become extremely divisive and filled with fear and anger. Some have even given up trying to talk to the other side and have blocked them from their conversations. Family members have stopped talking to each other and friends block each other on social media because of differences in political views. But I and some others still have hope. In January 2021, a historian colleague, Dr. Cristian Capotescu, and I wrote an opinion piece titled "Moving Forward in 2021: A Guide to Depolarizing America." There we made suggestions on how to try to reunite the country.

We believe an important step in this path is fighting the fear that is proliferated by politicians and the media (see next chapter), in order to overcome the resulting hate, division, and real and symbolic aggression. For that, we need to regain the ability to acknowledge and celebrate our collective achievements. We do that at a personal level with celebrating birthdays, job promotions, and graduations. We need that at a national and international level. We live in the safest and most prosperous age of humanity, far from wars and diseases that used to kill tens of millions of us on an ongoing basis. The resources and comforts that most Americans have today were dreams of kings a few decades ago. Science, technology, and medicine offer us new discoveries and solutions every day. AIDS is on its heels, and we are fighting infectious diseases better than we ever have. I do not mean to suggest that we do not have challenges, but things are not as dark as we are told they are. We need to recognize and appreciate these wins and achievements of our society, and humanity. In other words, we need to redefine our tribes based on common hopes, goals, needs, and strengths.

We need to seek out shared national and international common projects and goals that will allow us to see humanity as one with common needs. America needs to leave behind the zero-sum approach and begin to seek constructive projects that benefit Americans and the world regardless of political and tribal affiliations. We need to seek shared cultural, social, and political projects. For that, we must regain the ability of listening to the others, to the different in the spectrum of political and cultural discourse. That does not mean listening to the "others" through what our side of the media and politics selects for us. Those in the political and media spheres who have good intentions must become more serious about meaningful discourse. This means sharing respectful and leveled discussions of the political and cultural views with the public.

At a personal level, it is important to remember that regardless of what the tribe leaders and their media try to define for us, those who disagree with us are not enemies, stupid, or less human. It is still possible for a liberal and a conservative to go on a bike ride or have dinner together, and not hate each other because of the fate their leaders have determined for them. We also need to remember that not all of those who are in our corner are saints. If you believe all of what your party leaders say is the truth, and all of what the other side says is wrong, then you should think twice. It is impossible for one side of the argument to be always right, and for the other half of the country to be evil, wrong, or stupid.

This all requires hard work, but it is not impossible. And we do not have a better choice. The other option is to succumb to fatalism and hate, waiting for our society to collapse. More importantly, freedom from what others determine us to be, and the way others want us to see ourselves, others, and the world, is a very precious thing. It is one of the most important things that differentiates us from the other animals.

In the next chapter I will discuss the role that the media plays in division and fear, and how to protect ourselves from that, and from digital tribalism.

Chapter 15

The Business of Fear

The more the media peddled fear, the more the people lost the ability to believe in one another. For every new ill that befell them, the media created an explanation, and the explanation always had a face and a name. The people came to fear even their closest neighbors. At the level of the individual, the community, and the nation, people sought signs of others' ill intentions; and everywhere they looked, they found them, for this is what looking does.

—Bernard Beckett, New Zealand writer

On March 22, 2017, a man drove his car into the pedestrians outside the Palace of Westminster in London, killing five people and injuring around fifty. I remember on that day I was listening to the BBC in my car. With their usual emotionally neutral tone of voice, a reporter was sharing the facts about that attack. I switched to CNN and Fox News right away to hear their coverage of the same story. What immediately caught my attention was a dramatic shift in the tone in sharing the news: highly dramatic and emotional. Later, I looked at some of the same three outlets' headlines about the terrorist attack, and noticed the same contrast:

BBC: "Five People Killed in Westminster Terror Attack"
CNN: "Deadly Attack Leaves London Shaken"
Fox News: "London Suffers Worst Terrorist Attack in a Decade"

Imagine yourself living in London, at the time of the event. How would you feel differently about your safety in reaction to each of these headlines?

US cable news and media are uniquely different from serious news agencies in some other countries in that emotions play an important role in their work. Tucker Carlson on Fox News always looks angry, offended, and surprised by the "horrible things" he is sharing, and CNN's Wolf Blitzer always has a "very, very disturbing development" to report. Usually, watching the news for a couple of hours leaves viewers with a feeling that the whole world is going down in flames and that the US is on its path to total political and cultural destruction. The anchors and the commentators often choose a highly emotional tone, nonverbal behavior, and provocative words. The focus is more on the emotionally charged conclusion made by the people on TV, and much less so on what had really happened. As an Uber driver once told me, "The news that our parents watched was what happened; the news that we watch is what could possibly happen." The news pieces that are repeated over and over are mostly negative and worrisome, and the positive news stories are lower priority. In contrast, in some other countries, and to some extent our own publicly funded media, reporters are mostly dry and unemotional, and the words are about the "facts" and numbers. I put facts in quotations, because that unemotional nature does not necessarily mean honesty with the facts and information.

Another difference is the very narrow focus of the US media. In the rest of the world, you often see at least a couple of headlines about the most important developments across the world. But US cable news channels choose to repeat the same dramatically charged news item and their "analysis" over and over, at the cost of offering a very narrow view of the world and the US to their viewers. It is even hard to know how and why one specific topic was chosen for too broad of a coverage. Those who watched TV were hammered to boredom with minute-by-minute live coverage and analysis when Malaysian Airlines Flight 370 went missing in 2021. On CNN, you could barely see anything other than the latest development repeating itself over and over for almost a week. It was as if there was nothing else happening in the US or the world. And then the next shiny object took over and there was no mention of the flight anymore. As I am writing this chapter in late November 2022, there is a massive women's rights movement taking place in Iran. Iranians have come to the streets in masses after a twenty-two-year-old Iranian woman died in custody of the moral police. The protests have been happening every day since mid-September when they started. At 6:00 p.m. on September 27, I could barely find a couple of headlines buried at the bottom of the CNN website news feed, and did not find any related story on the Fox News website. These protests started about a week after the passing of Queen Elizabeth. You could see the details of what was going on with the Queen's corgis, but nothing about Iran.

MEDIA, TRIBALISM, AND FEAR

Along with US politics, the media have also become more and more tribal, and at times sound like the official outlets of a political party. They each have created an "us" that includes themselves, their favorite political party and agenda, and their viewers, against "them." "Them" is the opposing media, their politicians, and the affiliated other half of the country. They promote the same zero-sum game that is being played in the world of politics. When you watch or read each of these outlets, you by default know that you will not see anything good about "them," whether it is their politicians or their astute followers. It is all about the horrifying things the other half is doing to the country and the world. They, however, share two things: advertisements (mostly focused on greed, or fear of loss of something you need help to keep), and negativity. The common message is: you need to be afraid! Think about it. When was the last time you heard a series of good news on cable prime time? When there is one piece of good news, it is followed by a "but"! Even when things seem good, you must worry that someone is going to take them away from you.

The negative attitude is not limited to the US. Looking at the political news in the US, Germany, and Australia, a group of researchers found that negative tone outweighs positive tone ten to one! Another report looking at American, German, Austrian, and Italian news TV campaign coverage between 2004 and 2006 found negative political news amounted to near half of the news coverage, while positive news ranged between 6 and 15 percent. Another interesting study published in 2021 explored Twitter posts of forty-four news organizations both left and right leaning. What they found was: (a) both left- and right-leaning media organizations expressed more negative than positive affect on Twitter, (b) there was no difference between them in the amount of negative vs. positive coverage, and (c) negative news garnered more user engagement, leading to larger spread of the negativity. So if you think your favorite media outlet is different, think again.

But why would they do that?

The answer is in their desperate need for more viewership. Major media outlets, before anything else, are corporations. For a corporation, revenue is the top priority, even above the product. The larger the viewership, and the longer the people watch or read, the higher the revenue. And grabbing people's attention has become more and more difficult in the extremely competitive sphere of too many players, especially with the recent rise of social media.

Coincidentally, earlier today I was interviewed by a reporter from one of the major US media outlets, who wanted to know why the viewers get attracted to the negative and bad news. The answer to that question is: emotions in general, and negative emotions specifically, better grab the attention of the viewers, and keep them around to watch, listen, and click. That is because of our brain's inherent tendency to prioritize what might be signaling danger over other matters. Something sounding to be a threat, or a signal about threat (as in news) to us and ours, can more easily hijack our full attention. This is more important in the age of explosion of content where each headline only has a split-second chance for grabbing the click before we scroll down or switch to another channel. The viewers are more likely to stick around longer or click when the shared content is highly emotional. As we trust our tribe members even more when scared, people will even more rely on their team's media outlet when fear is the foundation. This all causes a constant competition between media outlets, and even between their own programs, for stealing the attention of a larger number of viewers. The importance and role of revenue generation in this process may be one reason that publicly funded media outlets in the US and elsewhere, without the urgent pressure for larger viewership, have remained more traditional, less emotional, and more focused on the content.

DRAMATIC IS NEWSWORTHY

Early in 2021, I was interviewed by a reporter from a European radio who wanted to know about refugees' mental health. After the interview we were discussing US politics and media. I learned that he was asked by his outlet to do a report on the US congressional representative from Georgia, Marjorie Taylor Greene. That was right during drama related to her conduct dominating the news, especially on the Left. This reporter, however, refrained from doing it. His reason was praiseworthy. To him, this was not important news and serious journalism! In the grand scheme of policy making in Congress, that drama was not consequential. In both our views, the media are in part responsible for showcasing the loudest outliers regardless of their importance, or lack of. At the end of the day, the viewers' perception of what is happening in the country, and what is "important," is mostly influenced by what they are told and what is covered. Most of us do not live in DC and do not care enough to listen to all that happens in Congress during the day. What we are told happened that day, is what we think happened that day. What we are not told about, did not happen.

In one of my lectures on fear, politics, and media, I show a slide with photos of two Republican politicians to the usually majority left-leaning audience. I ask them to raise their hand if they know the people in the photos. One of them is Marjorie Taylor Greene, representative for Georgia's Fourteenth

Congressional District, for whom almost everybody raises their hand. The other person, no hands raised, is Iowa senator Joni Ernst, the vice chair of the Senate Republican Conference. This experiment is a sad example of how media's focus on the immaterial issues has led to an absurd education of the public. As a senator and a leader in her party, Ernst's views and accomplishments are more important. In a normal world, news about her work would be more widely shared with the public, but Ernst is not considered "newsworthy." This pattern of coverage not only poorly educates the public about the substantial issues, but also puts the irrelevant in the center of public attention. And the more the public knows about it, the more it will dominate the field.

Similar to what often happens in life, in the media business the content is not as important as the feeling and the emotion attached to it. If something is primed with negative affect, it draws our attention. The negativity could be in the selective focus (highlighting negative events and ignoring the positive), in the tone the news is shared (negative affect on Tucker's face, or "very, very disturbing" words used by Wolf), or a pessimistic interpretation and outlook of the events. This reality show style of emotionality has dominated the business so much that sometimes it is difficult, for example, to differentiate reporting presidential election debates from a WWE fight. After debates, pundits are so excited to tell us about how one candidate "gutted" or "ripped" another, or "landed a punch." Even analysis of the debates is often focused on how a candidate was able to embarrass another or corner them with a "gotcha" comment, and not much about the substance of the debate. And realistically, how much substance could even be in a one-minute response on a highly complicated political, economic, or international affairs topic? This inflammatory language is not limited to election times. On July 28, 2022, I scrolled through the Fox News website, and here are some of the words that were used in their headlines: showdown, hit back, torch, defiant, die, rotting, fire, gruesome, nightmare.

This dramatic, *disaster pornography* approach creates a skewed and unreal understanding of the safety and prosperity of their nation and the world for the viewers. Despite the difficulties and challenges of the modern day, we indeed live in one of the safest periods of humanity. But to the consumers of the media, it feels like this country—and for that matter, the whole world—is going down in flames. A study by the Pew Research Center in 2016 found that despite a double-digit decline in the rates of violent and property crime in the US since 2008, most voters believed that the crime rates had hiked during that time period. And there is not much blame on them. When you live in a small village, you can see things for yourself. But to understand how things are in a city of millions, or a country of 331 million, you get your data from TV or the newspapers you trust. It is like children with limited access to the real world outside their home, who rely on their parents to tell them how things are out there!

Another example is the way mass shootings are covered, compared to sporadic cases of gun violence. A mass shooting—in fact, each incident of death or injury by gun violence—is a grave tragedy. And I have written about and done many interviews on the devastating impact of gun violence on individuals and collective society. But the big wave of news coverage of gun violence almost exclusively happens when there is a mass shooting. Sporadic events are not considered newsworthy. Nearly half of the firearm-related deaths in the US are caused by suicide. Additionally, mass shootings that are highlighted by the media are a very small fraction of the deaths caused by firearm homicide. Throughout the year and aside from when mass shootings happen in public places, there is rarely a coverage of shootings and firearm-related death, or serious and meaningful debates on the issue. We never see thought leaders of the two sides of the gun debate have a serious, respectful, uninterrupted conversation about the issue, and possible solutions on TV. When a mass shooting is considered newsworthy, it dominates the media sphere for weeks (or days), and then there is silence until the next mass shooting. While it is understandable to cover a horrible tragedy, this seasonal approach does not put a constant pressure on policy makers to force them to take action.

One thing we know this type of coverage does is terrify people. The chance of falling victim to gun violence in a school is extremely low, and probably less than being caught in the middle of a street or sporadic shooting. But because of the way school shootings are covered, they scare people more. I see parents who are terrified of sending their children to school after each school shooting (of which unfortunately there are too many). What I do is to remind them that although there is a risk, and that it is appalling that these tragedies keep happening, the risk of it happening to their child is still extremely low. Then we work together to separate the drama from the facts to gain a realistic assessment of the risk and best ways of mitigating it.

HOW TO STAY INFORMED WITHOUT
LOSING OUR SANITY

As responsible citizens, it is important for us to stay informed about what is happening around us. It is also vital to protect the mental health of ourselves and our children from the exposure to repeated negativity. In an article published in 2022, I offer practical tips on how to mitigate the effects of ongoing exposure to negative news, images, and videos. Some of these recommendations are basically what I do to protect myself from the impact of frequent exposure to my traumatized patients' horrific stories. Here is a summary of that article:

First and most importantly, reduce exposure. You just need one hour of listening to your favorite anchor to know what that cable news channel will be talking about over the next twenty-four hours. There is no need for hours of watching and listening to the same sad or terrifying news. All my patients who decreased exposure felt much better; research also supports this observation. Be especially careful about what your children see. Depending on their developmental stage, they perceive it differently. For example, a young child may think the school shooting or war they are seeing on TV is happening nearby, or in their own school. When they see repeated coverage of the tragedy, they might think it is another independent incident.

Try to limit exposure to emotionally intense delivery of the news. This can be done by listening to reporters who share the news in a more composed and fact-based manner. If you can, read instead of watching. Finally, keep a balanced look at the news; do not get addicted to the negative. Do not forget to also read or listen to the positive news about art, science, and technology, to keep a balanced view. If you need to watch TV, there are movies, documentaries, and fun shows to watch. Remember, what you see will ultimately become your reality. Make sure your reality is balanced.

SOCIAL MEDIA, THE MATRIX

A few years ago, a friend convinced me to create an Instagram account. I started with following a few fitness-and-diet-related accounts. That led to seeing more fitness-related suggestions, some of which I followed, and this kept happening. Gradually I found my feed was showered with everything fitness related, superathletic models, people who transformed their bodies in six months, how an actor got ripped, and posts with captions like "6 Key Rules to Being Shredded." My Instagram digital world became a fitness gallery. I could now imagine how someone with less objective exposure to the real world, who might perceive their digital world as a representation of reality, would feel. If I believed what I saw was the real world, it meant that even though I was working out regularly, I was way behind in exercise, diet, and physique.

I had a similar experience with Twitter when I started using it during the 2020 election campaign. Given my left-leaning independent political view, I followed a few media outlets and people of relevant opinion. I then began following some of the suggested accounts. I saw what they liked and who liked their posts or interacted with them, and kept following. At some point, all posts on my Twitter feed were saying the same things. My exposure to the Right was to their craziest members and craziest or least favorable ideas, handpicked by those I followed or those they interacted with. I had joined Twitter's leftist digital tribe!

Readers who use social media should be familiar with these experiences.

Those of us who are old enough to know life before the Matrix—social media—remember how excited we were about the birth of platforms like Facebook. Being able to connect to friends and family we had lost touch with sounded great. Then we began to connect with those with shared experiences and interests, and Twitter and Instagram joined our lives. This however, quickly changed. Social media transformed into Frankenstein monsters, a mishmash of hundreds and thousands of people we have never met, unverified news one-liners, random pictures, attention seeking, self-adoration and self-pity, and random ads.

Never before have humans been exposed to such a vast yet shallow river of trivial information. In a few seconds, you might see pictures of a friend's wedding, murder news, political fights, puppies, fake news, graphic images of war, dramatized TMI, and selfies of random people. It in some way looks like a dream, or rather an incoherent nightmare. This continues to train our brains for short attention, ADHD on cocaine!

SOCIAL MEDIA AND DIGITAL TRIBALISM

Like traditional media, social media's business model is based on promoting content that maximizes engagement. Artificial intelligence (AI) determines what you see first, based on what is guessed to capture your interest and engagement most, and keeps you scrolling and liking. For that, they track your expressed interests, likes, follows, connections, content engagement, and the amount of time you spend on each item, to show you the most relevant content and advertisements. What you see is what was found to engage others determined to be like you, what you usually click, and what is recent. Like traditional media, negative emotions—particularly anger and impulsivity—gain better traction. The engaging nature of the negative content also leads to its disproportional proliferation. And it does not matter if it is facts or not.

There is not necessarily a malicious intent behind the way these algorithms work. They are just designed to follow a business model of maximum engagement. I compare them with the casinos: the more time you spend there, the more they benefit. In a casino, you do not see any windows or clocks, because you should not notice the passage of time. They are designed to encourage the animal inside us to keep pulling the lever and clicking the button in hope for reward. Social media needs to keep us scrolling and clicking, to generate revenue. Casinos bank on your money, social media on your time.

In the movie *The Matrix*, humans are turned into immobile battery cells to keep the machines alive. In our Matrix, humans are turned into revenue-generating scrollers and clickers.

You keep clicking and following down the rabbit hole and end up in a "digital tribe," an exaggerated, extreme caricature of what you might have liked. But it also trains your brain to think and see things the way the tribe does, because now this is your new world to which your brain has to adapt. Social media gradually defines your social context, who you are linked with and what you see. At some point, all you see will be content produced or liked by your digital tribe, posts that are too similar, and often shared by many people. And if so many people in your sphere, the tribe that you trust, believe the same thing, why shouldn't you? While you do not see that each one of those others are a victim of the same process that got you to that spot, you become a member of an extreme corner of liberalism or conservatism, climate activism or denial, religion or antireligion, and other ideologies. You will not see different or opposing views as it is not determined relevant to your liking by AI. You are in the land of Oz: everything is green and everybody sees it green. When you do not see any opposing argument to the tribe's belief, it becomes easy to believe the earth is flat and run by intergalactic lizards disguised as humans, and that cryptocurrency is the future of the world economy. When you do see something about other tribes, it is handpicked by your own tribemates, their heads on a spike. There is no grayscale in the world of digital tribes.

FEAR, HATE, AND THE DIGITAL TRIBE

Members of the digital tribe keep consuming the same content, and feeding one another the same handpicked news, analyses, and ideologies. I call this phenomenon "digital inbreeding." We know inbreeding often does not make healthy babies. The loudest and most extreme members of the tribe begin to police the border against entry of anything different. The "others" are kicked out of the tribe by getting blocked or removed, or silenced by peer pressure, and members are shamed against opening up to "the different." The tribe is scared of and hates the "others" about whose worst attributes it has heard, seen pictures of, and read one-liner headlines.

Even those who feed the tribe suffer from "celebrity digital inbreeding." They become too confident about their ideas as they see everybody else thinks alike. The celebrities also see the same content, the same world, and as a result come to the same conclusion. Political pundits keep echoing each other, and thinking: "If others think like me, then I should most probably be right!" And that leads to terrible predictions about the real world, which does not follow the rules of the digital tribes. I very well remember how many political pundits were caught off guard in 2020 when Joe Biden began very strong, and excelled to the front of the Democratic primaries. Exposed to the same virtual cable news and social media world of like-minded people, those pundits had envisioned he had little to no chance.

In a recent study, more than 60 percent of Americans reported having unfriended, unfollowed, or blocked someone on social media because of their political views or posts. Unless by the time you are reading this book things have changed, you can probably relate to this. If you are politically engaged, how many Facebook friends do you still have from the other side of the political or ideological aisle? How many political leaders or thinkers from the other side do you follow on social media? How much original information (not handpicked by your tribe members) do you get from the other side? How many people have you unfriended or blocked due to their different beliefs?

By isolating us from real-life social connections, the recent pandemic expedited the dominance of the Matrix. For many people, the only source of information—and the only window to the outside world—has become social media. I often see people in and outside of my clinical practice who do not communicate with anyone other than those on their social media. Gradually, that becomes their real world. Before the Matrix, we knew people of other political affiliations or beliefs were still Americans who enjoyed Thanksgiving dinner with us. Now, all we know about the "different" and the "others" is what is fed to us by our digital tribe, and amplified by the AI algorithms. The negative and the fear consolidate each digital tribe against the "others." The Matrix is already here!

WHEN AFRAID, WE LOOK FOR MORE FEAR

A result of constant exposure to negative and scary posts, images, news, and analyses is keeping people in a heightened state of arousal and on the lookout for other scary things and bad news. Our emotions guide and redirect our attention. When scared or in a potentially dangerous situation, we are automatically more agile and prepared for fight or flight. This is an evolutionary response built to protect us in the situations of ongoing danger like war. Our attention scans the environment for threat and ignores the neutral and the positive.

The same happens to our attention in the digital sphere when we are constantly seeing bad news or suggestions that others are out there to get us or hurt our tribe. Scared people will even overinterpret the negativity of other news and posts and see what used to be neutral through the lens of bad news. They become more paranoid. Any statistics about the current state of the economy, foreign affairs, crime rates, or any action or words by "them" will be interpreted negatively. People also tend to overreact when scared; fear is impulsive because it has to be fast. Their responses to anything different or potentially opposing of their tribe's views is disproportional. In the time of war, you must be rough with the enemy. At the time of digital tribal war, you more easily and rapidly get into fights and lash out at others, and block and remove. Does that sound familiar?

IS THERE A RED PILL?

In the movie, Neo has to make the difficult choice between continuing the easy life in the colorful world of the Matrix, or taking the red pill and joining the more challenging real world. Many of us, especially those who were born in the era of social media, face the same choice throughout our day. Taking the blue pill will keep us in the shiny and easy scrolling world of algorithms and digital tribalism, and the red pill brings us back to the less comfortable reality. For those who are willing to take the red pill, what I suggested earlier in this chapter about protecting ourselves against bad news also applies here. Here are some more tips:

Review and update your preferences on your social media apps. You can confuse the AI algorithm by flagging the ads, regardless of relevance, as "irrelevant." Try to be more inclusive, stop blocking and unfriending and unfollowing, step outside of your digital tribe. The real world is not black and white; those who disagree with your political views are not evil. Add and follow respected thinkers and news sources, from outside of your tribe, and check out less politically biased and fact-based news sources, and non-for-profit outlets. An example is The Conversation (https://theconversation.com/us), a nonprofit outlet that shares with the public scholarly work written by academic experts on the major topics of the day. Find sources that focus on the news, and not their "interpretation." The "boring" news sources are the better ones; leave behind the negative thrill of the world of "breaking news." Try to go offline and have phone-free hours during the day; do not stay in this digital casino all day long. To avoid constant exposure, offload social media apps from your phone, and only check them on your computer at specific times of the day. Finally, try to engage in *real* social communications with real people outside the digital social networks.

In the movie *Mr. Nobody*, Nemo says: "I'm not afraid of dying. I'm afraid I haven't been alive enough."

Living in the real world is not as easy, but it is a lot more fulfilling. Don't be afraid.

Bibliography

CHAPTER 1

Duval, E. R., A. Javanbakht, and I. Liberzon. "Neural Circuits in Anxiety and Stress Disorders: A Focused Review." *Therapeutics and Clinical Risk Management* 11 (2015): 115–26. https://doi.org/10.2147/TCRM.S48528. https://www.ncbi.nlm.nih.gov/pubmed/25670901.

Maren, S., K. L. Phan, and I. Liberzon. "The Contextual Brain: Implications for Fear Conditioning, Extinction and Psychopathology." *Nature Reviews Neuroscience* 14, no. 6 (June 2013): 417–28. https://doi.org/10.1038/nrn3492. https://www.ncbi.nlm.nih.gov/pubmed/23635870.

Mobbs, D., R. Adolphs, M. S. Fanselow, L. F. Barrett, J. E. LeDoux, K. Ressler, and K. M. Tye. "Viewpoints: Approaches to Defining and Investigating Fear." *Nature Neuroscience* 22, no. 8 (August 2019): 1205–16. https://doi.org/10.1038/s41593-019-0456-6. https://www.ncbi.nlm.nih.gov/pubmed/31332374.

Roelofs, K. "Freeze for Action: Neurobiological Mechanisms in Animal and Human Freezing." *Philosophical Transactions of the Royal Society B: Biological Sciences* 372, no. 1718 (April 19, 2017). https://doi.org/10.1098/rstb.2016.0206. https://www.ncbi.nlm.nih.gov/pubmed/28242739.

Shin, L. M., and I. Liberzon. "The Neurocircuitry of Fear, Stress, and Anxiety Disorders." *Neuropsychopharmacology* 35, no. 1 (January 2010): 169–91. https://doi.org/10.1038/npp.2009.83. https://www.ncbi.nlm.nih.gov/pubmed/19625997.

Silva, B. A., C. T. Gross, and J. Graff. "The Neural Circuits of Innate Fear: Detection, Integration, Action, and Memorization." *Learning & Memory* 23, no. 10 (October 2016): 544–55. https://doi.org/10.1101/lm.042812.116. https://www.ncbi.nlm.nih.gov/pubmed/27634145.

Vahratian A., S. J. Blumberg, E. P. Terlizzi, and J. S. Schiller. "Symptoms of Anxiety or Depressive Disorder and Use of Mental Health Care among Adults during the COVID-19 Pandemic—United States, August 2020–February 2021." *Morbidity and Mortality Weekly Report* 70, no. 13, (April 2, 2021): 490–94. https://doi.org/10.15585/mmwr.mm7013e2. PMID: 33793459; PMCID: PMC8022876.

CHAPTER 2

Bowers, M. E., and K. J. Ressler. "An Overview of Translationally Informed Treatments for Posttraumatic Stress Disorder: Animal Models of Pavlovian Fear Conditioning to Human Clinical Trials." *Biological Psychiatry* 78, no. 5 (September 1, 2015): E15–27. https://doi.org/10.1016/j.biopsych.2015.06.008. https://www.ncbi.nlm.nih.gov/pubmed/26238379.

Hartley, C. A., and E. A. Phelps. "Changing Fear: The Neurocircuitry of Emotion Regulation." *Neuropsychopharmacology* 35, no. 1 (January 2010): 136–46. https://doi.org/10.1038/npp.2009.121. https://www.ncbi.nlm.nih.gov/pubmed/19710632.

Hermans, D., M. G. Craske, S. Mineka, and P. F. Lovibond. "Extinction in Human Fear Conditioning." *Biological Psychiatry* 60, no. 4 (August 15, 2006): 361–68. https://doi.org/10.1016/j.biopsych.2005.10.006. https://www.ncbi.nlm.nih.gov/pubmed/16503330.

Javanbakht, A., A. P. King, G. W. Evans, J. E. Swain, M. Angstadt, K. L. Phan, and I. Liberzon. "Childhood Poverty Predicts Adult Amygdala and Frontal Activity and Connectivity in Response to Emotional Faces." *Frontiers in Behavioral Neuroscience* 9 (2015): 154. https://doi.org/10.3389/fnbeh.2015.00154. https://www.ncbi.nlm.nih.gov/pubmed/26124712.

LeDoux, J. "The Emotional Brain, Fear, and the Amygdala." *Cellular and Molecular Neurobiology* 23, nos. 4–5 (October 2003): 727–38. https://doi.org/10.1023/a:1025048802629. https://www.ncbi.nlm.nih.gov/pubmed/14514027.

Menon, V., and L. Q. Uddin. "Saliency, Switching, Attention and Control: A Network Model of Insula Function." *Brain Structure and Function* 214, nos. 5–6 (June 2010): 655–67. https://doi.org/10.1007/s00429-010-0262-0. https://www.ncbi.nlm.nih.gov/pubmed/20512370.

CHAPTER 3

Alshak, M. N., and J. M. Das. "Neuroanatomy, Sympathetic Nervous System." In *StatPearls*. Treasure Island, FL, 2022.

Gothard, K. M. "The Amygdalo-motor Pathways and the Control of Facial Expressions." *Frontiers in Neuroscience* 8 (2014): 43. https://doi.org/10.3389/fnins.2014.00043. https://www.ncbi.nlm.nih.gov/pubmed/24678289.

Hughes, K., M. A. Bellis, K. A. Hardcastle, D. Sethi, A. Butchart, C. Mikton, L. Jones, and M. P. Dunne. "The Effect of Multiple Adverse Childhood Experiences on Health: A Systematic Review and Meta-analysis." *Lancet Public Health* 2, no. 8 (August 2017): e356–66. https://doi.org/10.1016/S2468-2667(17)30118-4. https://www.ncbi.nlm.nih.gov/pubmed/29253477.

Javanbakht, A., E. R. Duval, M. E. Cisneros, S. F. Taylor, D. Kessler, and I. Liberzon. "Instructed Fear Learning, Extinction, and Recall: Additive Effects of Cognitive Information on Emotional Learning of Fear." *Cognition and Emotion* 31, no. 5 (August 2017): 980–87. https://doi.org/10.1080/02699931.2016.1169997. https://www.ncbi.nlm.nih.gov/pubmed/27089509.

Javanbakht, A., L. R. Grasser, S. Kim, C. L. Arfken, and N. Nugent. "Perceived Health, Adversity, and Posttraumatic Stress Disorder in Syrian and Iraqi Refugees." *International Journal of Social Psychiatry* 68, no. 1 (February 2022): 118–28. https://doi.org/10.1177/0020764020978274. https://www.ncbi.nlm.nih.gov/pubmed/33269642.

Jovanovic, T., M. Keyes, A. Fiallos, K. M. Myers, M. Davis, and E. J. Duncan. "Fear Potentiation and Fear Inhibition in a Human Fear-Potentiated Startle Paradigm." *Biological Psychiatry* 57, no. 12 (June 15, 2005): 1559–64. https://doi.org/10.1016/j.biopsych.2005.02.025. https://www.ncbi.nlm.nih.gov/pubmed/15953493.

Preckel, D., and R. von Kanel. "Regulation of Hemostasis by the Sympathetic Nervous System: Any Contribution to Coronary Artery Disease?" *Heartdrug* 4, no. 3 (2004): 123–30. https://doi.org/10.1159/000078415. https://www.ncbi.nlm.nih.gov/pubmed/19169370.

Roelofs, K. "Freeze for Action: Neurobiological Mechanisms in Animal and Human Freezing." *Philosophical Transactions of the Royal Society B: Biological Sciences* 372, no. 1718 (April 19, 2017). https://doi.org/10.1098/rstb.2016.0206. https://www.ncbi.nlm.nih.gov/pubmed/28242739.

Tindle, J., and P. Tadi. "Neuroanatomy, Parasympathetic Nervous System." In *StatPearls*. Treasure Island, FL, 2022.

CHAPTER 4

Cook, M., and S. Mineka. "Observational Conditioning of Fear to Fear-Relevant versus Fear-Irrelevant Stimuli in Rhesus Monkeys." *Journal of Abnormal Psychology* 98, no. 4 (November 1989): 448–59. https://doi.org/10.1037//0021-843x.98.4.448. https://www.ncbi.nlm.nih.gov/pubmed/2592680.

Debiec, J., and R. M. Sullivan. "Intergenerational Transmission of Emotional Trauma through Amygdala-Dependent Mother-to-Infant Transfer of Specific Fear." *PNAS* 111, no. 33 (August 19, 2014): 12222–27. https://doi.org/10.1073/pnas.1316740111. https://www.ncbi.nlm.nih.gov/pubmed/25071168.

Deltomme, B., G. Mertens, H. Tibboel, and S. Braem. "Instructed Fear Stimuli Bias Visual Attention." *Acta Psychologica* 184 (March 2018): 31–38. https://doi.org/10.1016/j.actpsy.2017.08.010. https://www.ncbi.nlm.nih.gov/pubmed/28889903.

Dunsmoor, J. E., A. J. White, and K. S. LaBar. "Conceptual Similarity Promotes Generalization of Higher Order Fear Learning." *Learning & Memory* 18, no. 3 (2011): 156–60. https://doi.org/10.1101/lm.2016411. https://www.ncbi.nlm.nih.gov/pubmed/21330378.

Grasser, L. R., and T. Jovanovic. "Safety Learning during Development: Implications for Development of Psychopathology." *Behavioural Brain Research* 408 (June 25, 2021): 113297. https://doi.org/10.1016/j.bbr.2021.113297. https://www.ncbi.nlm.nih.gov/pubmed/33862062.

Javanbakht, A. "A Theory of Everything: Overlapping Neurobiological Mechanisms of Psychotherapies of Fear and Anxiety Related Disorders." *Frontiers in Behavioral*

Neuroscience 12 (2018): 328. https://doi.org/10.3389/fnbeh.2018.00328. https://www.ncbi.nlm.nih.gov/pubmed/30670956.

Javanbakht, A., E. R. Duval, M. E. Cisneros, S. F. Taylor, D. Kessler, and I. Liberzon. "Instructed Fear Learning, Extinction, and Recall: Additive Effects of Cognitive Information on Emotional Learning of Fear." *Cognition and Emotion* 31, no. 5 (August 2017): 980–87. https://doi.org/10.1080/02699931.2016.1169997. https://www.ncbi.nlm.nih.gov/pubmed/27089509.

Javanbakht, A., L. R. Grasser, S. Madaboosi, A. Chowdury, I. Liberzon, and V. A. Diwadkar. "The Neurocircuitry Underlying Additive Effects of Safety Instruction on Extinction Learning." *Frontiers in Behavioral Neuroscience* 14 (2020): 576247. https://doi.org/10.3389/fnbeh.2020.576247. https://www.ncbi.nlm.nih.gov/pubmed/33510623.

Javanbakht, A., D. Rosenberg, L. Haddad, and C. L. Arfken. "Mental Health in Syrian Refugee Children Resettling in the United States: War Trauma, Migration, and the Role of Parental Stress." *Journal of the American Academy of Child & Adolescent Psychiatry* 57, no. 3 (March 2018): 209–11 e2. https://doi.org/10.1016/j.jaac.2018.01.013. https://www.ncbi.nlm.nih.gov/pubmed/29496130.

LoBue, V., and J. S. DeLoache. "Superior Detection of Threat-Relevant Stimuli in Infancy." *Developmental Science* 13, no. 1 (January 1, 2010): 221–28. https://doi.org/10.1111/j.1467-7687.2009.00872.x. https://www.ncbi.nlm.nih.gov/pubmed/20121878.

Madaboosi, S., L. R. Grasser, A. Chowdury, and A. Javanbakht. "Neurocircuitry of Contingency Awareness in Pavlovian Fear Conditioning." *Cognitive, Affective & Behavioral Neuroscience* 21, no. 5 (October 2021): 1039–53. https://doi.org/10.3758/s13415-021-00909-6. https://www.ncbi.nlm.nih.gov/pubmed/33990933.

Ohman, A., A. Flykt, and F. Esteves. "Emotion Drives Attention: Detecting the Snake in the Grass." *Journal of Experimental Psychology: General* 130, no. 3 (September 2001): 466–78. https://doi.org/10.1037//0096-3445.130.3.466. https://www.ncbi.nlm.nih.gov/pubmed/11561921.

Olsson, A., K. I. Nearing, and E. A. Phelps. "Learning Fears by Observing Others: The Neural Systems of Social Fear Transmission." *Social Cognitive and Affective Neuroscience* 2, no. 1 (March 2007): 3–11. https://doi.org/10.1093/scan/nsm005. https://www.ncbi.nlm.nih.gov/pubmed/18985115.

Olsson, A., and E. A. Phelps. "Learned Fear of 'Unseen' Faces after Pavlovian, Observational, and Instructed Fear." *Psychological Science* 15, no. 12 (December 2004): 822–88. https://doi.org/10.1111/j.0956-7976.2004.00762.x. https://www.ncbi.nlm.nih.gov/pubmed/15563327.

Park, S. C. "Role of Putative Epigenetic Mechanisms in the Intergenerational Transmission of Trauma Effects in 'Comfort Women' Survivor Offspring." *Psychiatry Investigation* 16, no. 6 (June 2019): 475–76. https://doi.org/10.30773/pi.2019.05.01. https://www.ncbi.nlm.nih.gov/pubmed/31247708.

Raio, C. M., D. Carmel, M. Carrasco, and E. A. Phelps. "Nonconscious Fear Is Quickly Acquired but Swiftly Forgotten." *Current Biology* 22, no. 12 (June 19, 2012): R477–79. https://doi.org/10.1016/j.cub.2012.04.023. https://www.ncbi.nlm.nih.gov/pubmed/22720676.

Ren, C., and Q. Tao. "Neural Circuits Underlying Innate Fear." *Advances in Experimental Medicine and Biology* 1284 (2020): 1–7. https://doi.org/10.1007/978 -981-15-7086-5_1. https://www.ncbi.nlm.nih.gov/pubmed/32852735.

Seligman, M. E. "Phobias and Preparedness." *Behavior Therapy* 2 (1971): 307–20.

CHAPTER 6

Adolphs, R., D. Tranel, S. Hamann, A. W. Young, A. J. Calder, E. A. Phelps, A. Anderson, G. P. Lee, and A. R. Damasio. "Recognition of Facial Emotion in Nine Individuals with Bilateral Amygdala Damage." *Neuropsychologia* 37, no. 10 (September 1999): 1111–17. https://doi.org/10.1016/s0028-3932(99)00039-1. https://www.ncbi.nlm.nih.gov/pubmed/10509833.

Antoniadis, E. A., J. T. Winslow, M. Davis, and D. G. Amaral. "The Nonhuman Primate Amygdala Is Necessary for the Acquisition but Not the Retention of Fear-Potentiated Startle." *Biological Psychiatry* 65, no. 3 (February 1, 2009): 241–48. https://doi.org/10.1016/j.biopsych.2008.07.007. https://www.ncbi.nlm.nih .gov/pubmed/18823878.

Feinstein, J. S., R. Adolphs, A. Damasio, and D. Tranel. "The Human Amygdala and the Induction and Experience of Fear." *Current Biology* 21, no. 1 (January 11, 2011): 34–48. https://doi.org/10.1016/j.cub.2010.11.042. https://www.ncbi.nlm.nih .gov/pubmed/21167712.

Franco, Z. E., Blau, K., and P. G. Zimbardo. "Heroism: A Conceptual Analysis and Differentiation between Heroic Action and Altruism." *Review of General Psychology* 15 (2011): 99–113.

Goldstein, R. "Hugh Thompson, 62, Who Saved Civilians at My Lai, Dies." *New York Times*, January 7, 2006, http://www.nytimes.com/2006/01/07/national/07thompson .html?_r=0.

Oquendo, M. A., and J. J. Mann. "The Biology of Impulsivity and Suicidality." *Psychiatric Clinics of North America* 23, no. 1 (March 2000): 11–25. https:// doi.org/10.1016/s0193-953x(05)70140-4. https://www.ncbi.nlm.nih.gov/pubmed /10729928.

Pishnamazi, M., A. Tafakhori, S. Loloee, A. Modabbernia, V. Aghamollaii, B. Bahrami, and J. S. Winston. "Attentional Bias Towards and Away from Fearful Faces Is Modulated by Developmental Amygdala Damage." *Cortex* 81 (August 2016): 24–34. https://doi.org/10.1016/j.cortex.2016.04.012. https://www.ncbi.nlm .nih.gov/pubmed/27173975.

Putman, D. A. *Psychological Courage.* Lanham, MD: University Press of America, 2004.

Rachman, S. *Fear and Courage.* 2nd ed. New York: Freeman, 1990.

CHAPTER 7

Derntl, B., C. Windischberger, S. Robinson, I. Kryspin-Exner, R. C. Gur, E. Moser, and U. Habel. "Amygdala Activity to Fear and Anger in Healthy Young Males Is Associated with Testosterone." *Psychoneuroendocrinology* 34, no. 5 (June 2009): 687–93. https://doi.org/10.1016/j.psyneuen.2008.11.007. https://www.ncbi.nlm.nih.gov/pubmed/19136216.

DuPont-Reyes, M. J., D. Fry, V. I. Rickert, D. L. Bell, N. Palmetto, and L. L. Davidson. "Relationship Violence, Fear, and Exposure to Youth Violence among Adolescents in New York City." *Journal of Interpersonal Violence* 29, no. 12 (August 2014): 2325–50. https://doi.org/10.1177/0886260513518433. https://www.ncbi.nlm.nih.gov/pubmed/24457218.

Galambos, N. L., and R. A. Dixon. "Adolescent Abuse and the Development of Personal Sense of Control." *Child Abuse & Neglect* 8, no. 3 (1984): 285–93. https://doi.org/10.1016/0145-2134(84)90068-1. https://www.ncbi.nlm.nih.gov/pubmed/6383573.

Giovenardi, M., M. S. de Azevedo, S. P. da Silva, E. Hermel Edo, C. M. Gomes, and A. B. Lucion. "Neonatal Handling Increases Fear and Aggression in Lactating Rats." *Physiology & Behavior* 86, nos. 1–2 (September 15, 2005): 209–17. https://doi.org/10.1016/j.physbeh.2005.07.011. https://www.ncbi.nlm.nih.gov/pubmed/16099482.

Guo, X., V. Egan, and J. Zhang. "Sense of Control and Adolescents' Aggression: The Role of Aggressive Cues." *Psych Journal* 5, no. 4 (December 2016): 263–74. https://doi.org/10.1002/pchj.151. https://www.ncbi.nlm.nih.gov/pubmed/28032475.

Javanbakht, A., A. P. King, G. W. Evans, J. E. Swain, M. Angstadt, K. L. Phan, and I. Liberzon. "Childhood Poverty Predicts Adult Amygdala and Frontal Activity and Connectivity in Response to Emotional Faces." *Frontiers in Behavioral Neuroscience* 9 (2015): 154. https://doi.org/10.3389/fnbeh.2015.00154. https://www.ncbi.nlm.nih.gov/pubmed/26124712.

Modecki, K. L., L. K. Murphy, and A. M. Waters. "Exposure to Violence and Neglect Images Differentially Influences Fear Learning and Extinction." *Biological Psychology* 151 (March 2020): 107832. https://doi.org/10.1016/j.biopsycho.2019.107832. https://www.ncbi.nlm.nih.gov/pubmed/31904403.

Pichon, S., B. de Gelder, and J. Grezes. "Two Different Faces of Threat. Comparing the Neural Systems for Recognizing Fear and Anger in Dynamic Body Expressions." *Neuroimage* 47, no. 4 (October 1, 2009): 1873–83. https://doi.org/10.1016/j.neuroimage.2009.03.084. https://www.ncbi.nlm.nih.gov/pubmed/19371787.

Rosell, D. R., and L. J. Siever. "The Neurobiology of Aggression and Violence." *CNS Spectrums* 20, no. 3 (June 2015): 254–79. https://doi.org/10.1017/S109285291500019X. https://www.ncbi.nlm.nih.gov/pubmed/25936249.

Stowers, L., P. Cameron, and J. A. Keller. "Ominous Odors: Olfactory Control of Instinctive Fear and Aggression in Mice." *Current Opinion in Neurobiology* 23, no. 3 (June 2013): 339–45. https://doi.org/10.1016/j.conb.2013.01.007. https://www.ncbi.nlm.nih.gov/pubmed/23415829.

van Rooij, S. J. H., R. D. Smith, A. F. Stenson, T. D. Ely, X. Yang, N. Tottenham, J. S. Stevens, and T. Jovanovic. "Increased Activation of the Fear Neurocircuitry in Children Exposed to Violence." *Depression and Anxiety* 37, no. 4 (April 2020): 303–12. https://doi.org/10.1002/da.22994. https://www.ncbi.nlm.nih.gov/pubmed /31951308.

CHAPTER 8

Bruhl, A. B., A. Delsignore, K. Komossa, and S. Weidt. "Neuroimaging in Social Anxiety Disorder: A Meta-Analytic Review Resulting in a New Neurofunctional Model." *Neuroscience & Biobehavioral Reviews* 47 (November 2014): 260–80. https://doi.org/10.1016/j.neubiorev.2014.08.003. https://www.ncbi.nlm.nih.gov/ pubmed/25124509.

Duval, E. R., A. Javanbakht, and I. Liberzon. "Neural Circuits in Anxiety and Stress Disorders: A Focused Review." *Therapeutics and Clinical Risk Management* 11 (2015): 115–26. https://doi.org/10.2147/TCRM.S48528. https://www.ncbi.nlm.nih .gov/pubmed/25670901.

Harvard Medical School. "National Comorbidity Survey (NCS)." 2017. https://www .hcp.med.harvard.edu/ncs/index.php.

Lazarov, A., D. Basel, S. Dolan, D. G. Dillon, D. A. Pizzagalli, and F. R. Schneier. "Increased Attention Allocation to Socially Threatening Faces in Social Anxiety Disorder: A Replication Study." *Journal of Affective Disorders* 290 (July 1, 2021): 169–77. https://doi.org/10.1016/j.jad.2021.04.063. https://www.ncbi.nlm.nih.gov/ pubmed/34000570.

Maoz, K., S. Eldar, J. Stoddard, D. S. Pine, E. Leibenluft, and Y. Bar-Haim. "Angry-Happy Interpretations of Ambiguous Faces in Social Anxiety Disorder." *Psychiatry Research* 241 (July 30, 2016): 122–27. https://doi.org/10.1016/j .psychres.2016.04.100. https://www.ncbi.nlm.nih.gov/pubmed/27173656.

Mathew, S. J., and S. Ho. "Etiology and Neurobiology of Social Anxiety Disorder." *Journal of Clinical Psychiatry* 67, Suppl 12 (2006): 9–13. https://www.ncbi.nlm .nih.gov/pubmed/17092190.

Stein, M. B., and D. J. Stein. "Social Anxiety Disorder." *Lancet* 371, no. 9618 (March 29, 2008): 1115–25. https://doi.org/10.1016/S0140-6736(08)60488-2. https://www .ncbi.nlm.nih.gov/pubmed/18374843.

Other Resources

Anxiety and Depression Association of America: https://adaa.org
Burns, David D. *Feeling Good.* 2nd ed. New York: Harper, 2000.

CHAPTER 9

Abu Suhaiban, H., L. R. Grasser, and A. Javanbakht. "Mental Health of Refugees and Torture Survivors: A Critical Review of Prevalence, Predictors, and Integrated Care." *International Journal of Environmental Research and Public Health* 16, no. 13 (June 28, 2019). https://doi.org/10.3390/ijerph16132309. https://www.ncbi.nlm .nih.gov/pubmed/31261840.

American Psychiatric Association, and American Psychiatric Association *DSM*-5 Task Force. *Diagnostic and Statistical Manual of Mental Disorders: DSM-5.* 5th ed. Washington, DC: American Psychiatric Association, 2013.

Duval, E. R., A. Javanbakht, and I. Liberzon. "Neural Circuits in Anxiety and Stress Disorders: A Focused Review." *Therapeutics and Clinical Risk Management* 11 (2015): 115–26. https://doi.org/10.2147/TCRM.S48528. https://www.ncbi.nlm.nih .gov/pubmed/25670901.

Gilbertson, M. W., M. E. Shenton, A. Ciszewski, K. Kasai, N. B. Lasko, S. P. Orr, and R. K. Pitman. "Smaller Hippocampal Volume Predicts Pathologic Vulnerability to Psychological Trauma." *Nature Neuroscience* 5, no. 11 (November 2002): 1242–47. https://doi.org/10.1038/nn958. https://www.ncbi.nlm.nih.gov/pubmed /12379862.

Grasser, L. R., B. Saad, C. Bazzi, C. Wanna, H. Abu Suhaiban, D. Mammo, T. Jovanovic, and A. Javanbakht. "Skin Conductance Response to Trauma Interview as a Candidate Biomarker of Trauma and Related Psychopathology in Youth Resettled as Refugees." *European Journal of Psychotraumatology* 13, no. 1 (2022): 2083375. https://doi.org/10.1080/20008198.2022.2083375. https://www .ncbi.nlm.nih.gov/pubmed/35713586.

Hartley, T. A., J. M. Violanti, K. Sarkisian, M. E. Andrew, and C. M. Burchfiel. "PTSD Symptoms among Police Officers: Associations with Frequency, Recency, and Types of Traumatic Events." *International Journal of Emergency Mental Health and Human Resilience* 15, no. 4 (2013): 241–53. https://www.ncbi.nlm.nih .gov/pubmed/24707587.

Hinrichs, R., S. J. van Rooij, V. Michopoulos, K. Schultebraucks, S. Winters, J. Maples-Keller, A. O. Rothbaum, et al. "Increased Skin Conductance Response in the Immediate Aftermath of Trauma Predicts PTSD Risk." *Chronic Stress (Thousand Oaks)* 3 (January–December 2019). https://doi.org/10.1177/2470547019844441. https://www.ncbi.nlm.nih.gov/pubmed/31179413.

Javanbakht, A., A. Amirsadri, H. Abu Suhaiban, M. I. Alsaud, Z. Alobaidi, Z. Rawi, and C. L. Arfken. "Prevalence of Possible Mental Disorders in Syrian Refugees Resettling in the United States Screened at Primary Care." *Journal of Immigrant and Minority Health* 21, no. 3 (June 2019): 664–67. https://doi.org/10.1007/s10903 -018-0797-3. https://www.ncbi.nlm.nih.gov/pubmed/30066059.

Javanbakht, A., I. Liberzon, A. Amirsadri, K. Gjini, and N. N. Boutros. "Event-Related Potential Studies of Post-traumatic Stress Disorder: A Critical Review and Synthesis." *Biology of Mood & Anxiety Disorders* 1, no. 1 (October 12, 2011): 5. https://doi.org/10.1186/2045-5380-1-5. https://www.ncbi.nlm.nih.gov/pubmed /22738160.

Saunders, B. E., and Z. W. Adams. "Epidemiology of Traumatic Experiences in Childhood." *Child and Adolescent Psychiatric Clinics of North America* 23, no. 2 (April 2014): 167–84, vii. https://doi.org/10.1016/j.chc.2013.12.003. https://www.ncbi.nlm.nih.gov/pubmed/24656575.

Other Resources

Rothbaum, B. O., and S. A. M. Rauch. *PTSD: What Everyone Needs to Know.* New York: Oxford University Press, 2020.
https://theconversation.com/syrian-refugees-in-america-the-forgotten-psychological-wounds-of-the-stress-of-migration-96155
https://theconversation.com/fireworks-can-torment-veterans-and-survivors-of-gun-violence-with-ptsd-heres-how-to-celebrate-with-respect-for-those-who-served-141731
https://theconversation.com/the-aching-blue-trauma-stress-and-invisible-wounds-of-those-in-law-enforcement-146539
https://theconversation.com/the-aching-red-firefighters-often-silently-suffer-from-trauma-and-job-related-stress-164994
https://theconversation.com/mass-shootings-leave-behind-collective-despair-anguish-and-trauma-at-many-societal-levels-183884
https://theconversation.com/brain-scans-help-shed-light-on-the-ptsd-brain-but-they-cannot-diagnose-ptsd-115669

CHAPTER 10

Grasser, L. R., and A. Javanbakht. "Virtual Arts and Movement Therapies for Youth in the Era of COVID-19." *Journal of the American Academy of Child & Adolescent Psychiatry* 60, no. 11 (November 2021): 1334–36. https://doi.org/10.1016/j.jaac.2021.06.017. https://www.ncbi.nlm.nih.gov/pubmed/34246787.

Javanbakht, A. "The Exercise Pill: How Exercise Keeps Your Brain Healthy and Protects It against Depression and Anxiety." The Conversation. February 25, 2021. https://theconversation.com/the-exercise-pill-how-exercise-keeps-your-brain-healthy-and-protects-it-against-depression-and-anxiety-155848.

Javanbakht, A., S. Madaboosi, and L. R. Grasser. "Real-Life Contextualization of Exposure Therapy Using Augmented Reality: A Pilot Clinical Trial of a Novel Treatment Method." *Annals of Clinical Psychiatry* 33, no. 4 (November 2021): 220–31. https://doi.org/10.12788/acp.0042. https://www.ncbi.nlm.nih.gov/pubmed/34672925.

Nader, K., G. E. Schafe, and J. E. Le Doux. "Fear Memories Require Protein Synthesis in the Amygdala for Reconsolidation after Retrieval." *Nature* 406, no. 6797 (August 17, 2000): 722–76. https://doi.org/10.1038/35021052. https://www.ncbi.nlm.nih.gov/pubmed/10963596.

CHAPTER 11

Gustafsson E., C. Francoeur, I. Blanchette, and S. Sirois. "Visual Exploration in Adults: Habituation, Mere Exposure, or Optimal Level of Arousal?" *Learning & Behavior* 50, no. 2 (2022): 233–41.

CHAPTER 12

Buhle, J. T., J. A. Silvers, T. D. Wager, R. Lopez, C. Onyemekwu, H. Kober, J. Weber, and K. N. Ochsner. "Cognitive Reappraisal of Emotion: A Meta-analysis of Human Neuroimaging Studies." *Cerebral Cortex* 24, no. 11 (November 2014): 2981–90. https://doi.org/10.1093/cercor/bht154. https://www.ncbi.nlm.nih.gov/pubmed/23765157.

Frankl, Viktor E. *Man's Search for Meaning: An Introduction to Logotherapy.* Boston: Beacon, 1962.

Fuentes-Sanchez, N., I. Jaen, M. A. Escrig, I. Lucas, and M. C. Pastor. "Cognitive Reappraisal during Unpleasant Picture Processing: Subjective Self-Report and Peripheral Physiology." *Psychophysiology* 56, no. 8 (August 2019): e13372. https://doi.org/10.1111/psyp.13372. https://www.ncbi.nlm.nih.gov/pubmed/30927456.

Hirschberger, G. "Collective Trauma and the Social Construction of Meaning." *Frontiers in Psychology* 9 (2018): 1441. https://doi.org/10.3389/fpsyg.2018.01441. https://www.ncbi.nlm.nih.gov/pubmed/30147669.

Javanbakht, A., L. R. Grasser, S. Madaboosi, A. Chowdury, I. Liberzon, and V. A. Diwadkar. "The Neurocircuitry Underlying Additive Effects of Safety Instruction on Extinction Learning." *Frontiers in Behavioral Neuroscience* 14 (2020): 576247. https://doi.org/10.3389/fnbeh.2020.576247. https://www.ncbi.nlm.nih.gov/pubmed/33510623.

Nelson, B. D., D. A. Fitzgerald, H. Klumpp, S. A. Shankman, and K. L. Phan. "Prefrontal Engagement by Cognitive Reappraisal of Negative Faces." *Behavioural Brain Research* 279 (February 15, 2015): 218–25. https://doi.org/10.1016/j.bbr.2014.11.034. https://www.ncbi.nlm.nih.gov/pubmed/25433095.

Updegraff, J. A., R. C. Silver, and E. A. Holman. "Searching for and Finding Meaning in Collective Trauma: Results from a National Longitudinal Study of the 9/11 Terrorist Attacks." *Journal of Personality and Social Psychology* 95, no. 3 (September 2008): 709–22. https://doi.org/10.1037/0022-3514.95.3.709. https://www.ncbi.nlm.nih.gov/pubmed/18729704.

CHAPTER 13

Becker, Ernest, and Ralph Ellison Collection (Library of Congress). *The Denial of Death.* New York: Free Press, 1973.

Sligte, D. J., B. A. Nijstad, and C. K. De Dreu. "Leaving a Legacy Neutralizes Negative Effects of Death Anxiety on Creativity." *Personality and Social Psychology Bulletin* 39, no. 9 (September 2013): 1152–63. https://doi.org/10.1177 /0146167213490804.

CHAPTER 14

Chiao, J. Y., T. Iidaka, H. L. Gordon, J. Nogawa, M. Bar, E. Aminoff, N. Sadato, and N. Ambady. "Cultural Specificity in Amygdala Response to Fear Faces." *Journal of Cognitive Neuroscience* 20, no. 12 (December 2008): 2167–74. https://doi.org/10 .1162/jocn.2008.20151. https://www.ncbi.nlm.nih.gov/pubmed/18457504.

Harada, T., Y. Mano, H. Komeda, L. A. Hechtman, N. Pornpattananangkul, T. B. Parrish, N. Sadato, T. Iidaka, and J. Y. Chiao. "Cultural Influences on Neural Systems of Intergroup Emotion Perception: An fMRI Study." *Neuropsychologia* 137 (February 3, 2020): 107254. https://doi.org/10.1016/j.neuropsychologia.2019 .107254. https://www.ncbi.nlm.nih.gov/pubmed/31726067.

Javanbakht, A., and C. Capotescu. "Moving Forward in 2021: A Guide to Depolarizing America." Psychology Today. January 4, 2021. https://www.psychologytoday.com /us/blog/the-many-faces-anxiety-and-trauma/202101/moving-forward-in-2021 -guide-depolarizing-america.

Javanbakht, A., A. Stenson, N. Nugent, A. Smith, D. Rosenberg, and T. Jovanovic. "Biological and Environmental Factors Affecting Risk and Resilience among Syrian Refugee Children." *Journal of Psychiatry and Brain Science* 6 (2021). https://doi.org/10.20900/jpbs.20210003. https://www.ncbi.nlm.nih.gov/pubmed /33791438.

Molenberghs, P., J. Gapp, B. Wang, W. R. Louis, and J. Decety. "Increased Moral Sensitivity for Outgroup Perpetrators Harming Ingroup Members." *Cerebral Cortex* 26, no. 1 (January 2016): 225–33. https://doi.org/10.1093/cercor/bhu195. https://www.ncbi.nlm.nih.gov/pubmed/25183886.

CHAPTER 15

Bellovary, A. K., N. A. Young, and A. Goldenberg. "Left- and Right-Leaning News Organizations Use Negative Emotional Content and Elicit User Engagement Similarly." *Affective Science* 2, no. 4 (2021): 391–96. https://doi.org/10.1007/ s42761-021-00046-w. https://www.ncbi.nlm.nih.gov/pubmed/34423311.

Goodwin, E. "The Majority of Americans Are Also Social Distancing from Politics." Civic Science. September 9, 2020. https://civicscience.com/the-majority -of-americans-are-also-social-distancing-from-politics/.

Gramlich, J. "Voters' Perceptions of Crime Continue to Conflict with Reality." Pew Research Center. 2016. https://www.pewresearch.org/fact-tank/2016/11/16/voters -perceptions-of-crime-continue-to-conflict-with-reality/.

Javanbakht, A. "How to Protect Your Family from Horrific News Images—and Still Stay Informed." The Conversation. April 28, 2022, https://theconversation.com/how-to-protect-your-family-from-horrific-news-images-and-still-stay-informed-181818.

Lengauer, G., F. Esser, and R. Berganza. "Negativity in Political News: A Review of Concepts, Operationalizations and Key Findings." *Journalism* 13, no. 2 (2011): 179–202.

Index

About the Author

Arash Javanbakht, MD, is a psychiatrist who currently serves as the director of the Stress, Trauma, and Anxiety Research Clinic (STARC) at Wayne State University School of Medicine. His research is focused on anxiety, trauma, and PTSD, and he treats civilians, refugees, and first responders who suffer from PTSD. Dr. Javanbakht is a frequently invited keynote speaker at national and international conferences as well as universities for his expertise in the subjects covered in this book. Multiple media outlets have featured Dr. Javanbakht's work, including CNN, National Geographic, *Aljazeera*, NPR, the *Washington Post*, Smithsonian, PBS, American Psychiatric Association Press Briefing, Anxiety and Depression Association of America, and the American Academy of Child and Adolescent Psychiatry. He is the academic advisor on the PBS documentary "Mysteries of Mental Illness." Dr. Javanbakht was recently nominated by Beth Daley, *The Conversation's* editor and general manager, for the American Academy for Advancement of Science Early Career Award for Public Engagement with Science.

Milton Keynes UK
Ingram Content Group UK Ltd.
UKHW041656301023
431602UK00006B/37